THE TRICK IS
IN THE TRAINING

THE TRICK IS IN THE TRAINING

Dozens of Fun Tricks to Teach Your Dog

Stephanie J. Taunton and Cheryl S. Smith

About the Authors
Stephanie J. Taunton, a state-certified dog trainer, is the director
and owner of Bow Wow Productions, an animal training facility
for the film, television, and print industry. Many of her animal
actors have been rescued from local animal shelters. In addition,
she is the curator of the Hesperia Zoo, which promotes education
with a large variety of wild animals.

Cheryl S. Smith is an award-winning pet writer, with books on
dog-human communication, dog-friendly gardens, dog showing,
and dog care and health. She broadcasts her radio show *PetSmith*
on station KONP and writes the nutrition column for *Dogs in
Canada* magazine. She has lectured across the United States,
Canada, and Japan, and appeared frequently on radio and television. At home, she trains her own dogs, chickens, and llamas.

All inquiries should be addressed to:
Barron's Educational Series, Inc.
250 Wireless Boulevard
Hauppauge, NY 11788
www.barronseduc.com

ISBN-13: 978-0-7641-4211-6
ISBN-10: 0-7641-4211-9

Library of Congress Catalog Card No. 2009033206

Library of Congress Cataloging-in-Publication Data

Taunton, Stephanie J.
    The trick is in the training / Stephanie J. Taunton and
Cheryl S. Smith. — 2nd ed.
        p. cm.
    Includes bibliographical references and index.
    ISBN-13: 978-0-7641-4211-6 (alk. paper)
    ISBN-10: 0-7641-4211-9 (alk. paper)
  1. Dogs—Training.   I. Smith, Cheryl S.   II. Title.
    SF431.T385 2010
    636.7'0835—dc22   2009033206

Printed in China
9 8 7 6 5 4 3 2 1

CONTENTS

ACKNOWLEDGMENTS

The authors would like to thank the following dog owners who allowed their dogs to participate in the book: Gypsy—Andrea SanFilippo, Bling Bling—Judy Cordromp, Apple and Ruby—Tina Roy, and Fly—Michelle Borchardt. Dogs owned by Stephanie Taunton: Dudley, T-Bone, Ricochet, Sky, Diesel, Bobby, DaVinci, Finnegan, Touché, Ketchup, Trouble, Matilda, Vegas, Clever, Bug, and Zane, and Harvey the cat. Our thanks also to the dog trainers and handlers: Jill and Leonard Hixson, Judy Cordromp, Tina Farias, and Kevin Cordromp "Boy Child." Thanks to Janet Alexander, Spa for Pets, Judy Winthrop for her suggestions and illustrations, and Serling and Diamond for getting Cheryl Smith involved with Stephanie Taunton.

To Sapir Weiss my mentor, who has helped me throughout my career with guidance and support. To my mom, for helping me and for encouraging me to follow my dreams. All my love!
—Stephanie J. Taunton

To my father, who taught me to seek my own solutions and to find a way through the world that suited me best. To all my dogs, who, each in his or her own way, forced me to seek a variety of solutions and learn to better understand another being.
—Cheryl S. Smith

CHAPTER 1
DOING WHAT COMES NATURALLY

As the title of the book indicates, what we will discuss here is how to teach what are usually thought of as "tricks" to your dog. That word "tricks" is misleading. All of the exercises you and your dog will learn here are based on natural behaviors or extensions of natural behaviors. What we will do is teach you how to train your dog to perform them on command. Rather than "trick training," we call this "animal acting." (This same strategy of training works equally well for many animals besides dogs. You can use these lessons to train your cat, horse, llama, or whatever—as long as your pet is food motivated, you can teach it some acting. Keep any physical limitations in mind—potbellied pigs are NOT good candidates for sitting up, and horses just WON'T crawl like a dog.)

Dogs act on their own just fine. If you're sitting and eating a nice juicy cheeseburger and your dog is watching, you can surely read the message in his pathetic, yearning eyes. Or jingle your car keys or pick up a leash and watch an exhibit of pure unadulterated joy. Using your dog's natural abilities and adding some training, you can have a dog that will look ashamed (*Head down*), excited (*Circle left/Circle right*), or apprehensive (*Where's your nose?*) on command.

You will also see your dog shine with new enthusiasm and intelligence. Dogs were bred to hunt, track, herd, guard, kill vermin, and pull carts. We rarely use these natural abilities. Animal acting will tap into these hidden talents and give your dog a more fulfilling station in life.

Harvey

Here is an example of a natural behavior. Dogs are always putting their front paws on all sorts of things and getting in all kinds of trouble for it. Ask any trainer of basic good manners classes what complaint he or she hears most, and you're sure to be told "jumping up." Now you can put that behavior to good use AND control when it happens. Jumping up will become *Feet up*, with you choosing the target.

Feet up can pose a dog beautifully for photographs, whether you're taking some snapshots for your own pleasure or a professional has decided your canine is calendar material. It's a very helpful behavior in pet therapy work—having a dog who will carefully put her feet

Dudley, Labrador Retriever

up on the side of a bed or the arm of a wheelchair helps patients with limited mobility give a pat or receive a kiss (another natural behavior easy to put on cue—see Chapter 10).

Feet up is also very useful when you *do* want the dog to get up on something. Most dogs too heavy to pick up easily can reach a grooming table or the tailgate of a pickup truck with their front feet. You can then just boost their back end up onto the table or into the truck, saving wear and tear on your back. The two-year-old that boings into a truck with scarcely a thought may be glad for a boost in eight or nine years. You'll be glad you taught *Feet up*.

Some of the behaviors included here are used in professional work all the time. Watch all those dog-inhabited commercials, TV shows, and movies and you'll probably see *Head down*, *Sit up*, and *Speak* more than once. If you're a "stage master" with acting aspirations for your best friend, having a repertoire of these behaviors on cue will certainly put you ahead of the pack. Other behaviors are rarely called for in professional circles, but may be a hit in convalescent hospital activity rooms or at county fair animal talent competitions. All are easily accomplished by the average dog and handler.

Practicing these behaviors should be FUN for you and your dog. Don't get all grim and uptight about it. Some take longer than others to perfect, and some dogs are better

Bling Bling, Papillon

*T-Bone,
Mixed Breed*

at one thing than another. Stars are generally made, not born. All dogs in good physical and mental condition should eventually master all of them. (And, not to lay all the blame on the dog, some handlers are naturally talented and some are just a bit klutzy. Follow the tips about timing and problem solving included with each of the behavior write-ups and you'll do fine.)

Animal acting creates a great bond between you and your dog. Especially if yours is not an active lifestyle, it will give you both a workout.

One important reminder—reward behaviors only when you have requested them or you will soon find your dog playing you like a finely tuned fiddle, cashing in on cookies whenever he wants. It may be really hard to ignore your dog when he places himself between you and the TV, looks you straight in the eye, and sits up and waves, but *you're* supposed to be the one in charge.

Odds are that your dog won't get a chance to show her stuff on camera or in print, though you never know—Chapter 3 gives some information on the world of the professional. But you WILL both have some fun, learn new things, and at the very least have something to show off on your walks in the park.

Ricochet, Dalmatian

CHAPTER 2
SO WHAT'S MY MOTIVATION?

In animal acting, we use a little of everything, whatever we need to elicit a particular behavior. But our most important tools are food rewards and praise, with some physical manipulation thrown in. We have tried to make it as easy as possible for you and your dog. With some behaviors we've provided two ways of doing things. We generally start with lure/reward, but if the dog is having a hard time understanding what you want, gently placing her into position and then rewarding can give you that "aha" moment and advance your training before your dog becomes frustrated. All you need to do is follow the instructions for each of the behaviors, paying close attention to the tips on timing and problem solving.

You need to know what best motivates your dog. Some dogs have strong food motivation, others have a strong prey drive, some will have both. Food motivation tends to be the easiest training method. Dogs with strong prey drives like to play with balls and squeaky toys, but it takes more time to reward them with play. If your dog likes both food and toys, you can try switching from one to the other when training a particular behavior to see which gets a better response.

Animal acting does use a substantial amount of food, especially when teaching new behaviors. If you have a dog who gains weight by merely sniffing food, you will need to plan how to avoid ending up with a well-trained but seriously obese dog.

Matilda, Basset Hound

If the dog eats anything any time, the simplest strategy is to use some of the dog's regular kibble as your training treat. Don't forget to deduct that amount from the dog's dinner bowl. You can even measure the dog's ration into the bowl in the morning, dip into it for your training sessions through the day, and feed whatever is left for dinner. Leaving food down for the dog all day will lower his food motivation and make it difficult to train some behaviors. A hungry dog is a motivated dog.

Some dogs just are not excited about their regular old kibble as a treat. There are literally hundreds of dog treats to choose from. You need to find a treat that your dog finds exciting, that can be eaten quickly, and that can be tossed over some distance to your dog. Tossing a treat keeps the dog at a distance waiting for the treat rather than moving toward you. A bait bag or fanny pack will give you a convenient, accessible place to keep your treats while training.

The timing of your reward is extremely important, so much so that each set of behavior instructions in the book includes a quick section specifying when to give the dog the treat. Incorrect timing means you are not rewarding the correct action, or, in other words, not training what you think you're training. If your dog sits up beautifully but your reward always comes when her front feet are back on the ground, she may think the action you are after is a quick "Sit up, sit down" sequence. Always consider what you are rewarding. Associate the command with the action with the reward.

Many people use a technique called clicker training to deal with timing issues. The clicker, usually a small plastic rectangle with a metal strip, makes a "click clack" sound when the metal strip is depressed and released. If you have trouble getting the treat to your dog while the desired behavior is still occurring, you can use the clicker to "mark" the behavior, then deliver the treat. The dog will learn, through repetition, that the behavior happening when the click occurs is what is being rewarded. (For more on clicker training, read *Quick Clicks* by Mandy Book and Cheryl S. Smith.)

Practice a new behavior for no more than ten or fifteen minutes at a time, two or three times a day. Some behaviors may start to shape up nicely after only a couple of days; others may take weeks. Don't get discouraged. Check your timing and read the problem-solving tips if you seem to be stalled.

As your dog becomes more accomplished at a behavior, you should offer food less often. If you continue to reward every performance, quality will gradually deteriorate. The dog will do as little as possible to receive the reward. Once a behavior is learned, you reward at random or choose only the best performances to reward. This sporadic pay-off keeps the dog working to earn his reward, the same as the payout from a slot machine keeps you putting in more coins. When your dog is proficient in many behaviors, ask him to perform several before he's rewarded with food. Or ask him to

Ketchup, Norwich Terrier

Vegas, Golden Retriever

"Stay" in a position. Note that once you use a *Stay*, you also need a *Release*, to let your dog know you are ending the command. Always remember to release the dog from a stay, or he will learn to release himself and your stay will have no power. Common release cues include "Free," "All done," "Take a break," and "Release."

Food is not the only reward, of course. Your praise should also be valuable to your dog. This is not likely to be the case if your praise consists of a monotone, "Good boy." Your praise needs to be genuine and enthusiastic. Here, too, you need to learn what motivates your dog. With a high-energy, totally keyed-in dog, a simple "Good dog" may be enough. But the average dog requires more. You may, in fact, need to use a high, squeaky voice, gyrate like a cheerleader, and behave in a way that makes you feel like a complete fool. This is your performance for your dog.

Learn what works best with your dog and use it to your advantage.

While teaching a behavior, you use both a command and a rough version of a signal. You use your hand movement to lure the dog into position, say the command to associate it with the action, and reward the desired behavior (or sometimes some portion of a more complex behavior). Once the behavior is learned, you should be able to use a command alone, a signal alone, or both together. Your performance is often more impressive if you use just signals, as your audience may not even be aware that you are cuing the dog.

Hand signals can be difficult to describe or even show in photographs, as most of them involve movement. They are based on the movements you make while teaching the dog a behavior. So the sweep of your hand up and back over the dog's head to lure him into a *Sit up* becomes the same up-and-out hand movement used even when you are standing up and signaling a dog ten feet away once the behavior is learned. The signals shown here are fairly standard in the professional animal acting business and used by most of the handlers. But it is not important that you copy them exactly. You can use whatever works for you, as long as the dog can see a signal and recognize what it means.

How well you will be able to use physical manipulation depends on the trust you have developed with your dog. All dogs should accept handling just for ease in everyday life. Putting drops in eyes, cleaning ears, and trimming toenails should not be life-and-death struggles. Any good puppy care book instructs owners to play with their puppy's feet, ears, and mouth. If you have neglected this important detail of dog ownership until now, start immediately. Even if your dog is no longer a puppy, you can do this. Your relationship with your dog should be based on trust, and a dog that trusts you should accept handling, even if he doesn't like it. In fact, if you want to see some real natural acting ability, check out the heart-wrenching pathos of a reluctant dog having his nails clipped.

CHAPTER 3
STRUTTIN' YOUR STUFF

If you harbor a desire to have your dog become the next Lassie, Benji, or Eddie, we've got to tell you it's not very likely. There just aren't that many recurring starring roles out there. But there are plenty of opportunities to strut your stuff, and some of them will make you money. Just not enough to retire on.

FAME . . .

If you have not tried the pet therapy work mentioned frequently throughout this book, you may want to look into it. You can bring joy to the residents of convalescent hospitals or a smile to a hospital's pediatric ward. It is a highly rewarding volunteer activity, and you and your performing pooch can gain plenty of experience. Check with your local humane society or kennel club to see if they have a program active in your area, or contact one of the national organizations promoting this activity (see Useful Addresses, page 101). It's an excellent opportunity to hone your act. And though you can visit on your own, if you are certified by one of the national organizations, you will be covered by their liability insurance coverage whenever you go on a visit.

If you visit without a group, be aware that there are guidelines. Your dog must be clean and flea-free. He or she should be friendly but not boisterous. You must not inflict any scratches on patients, however unintentional they may be. You will need to get permission from someone at the facility before you begin your visits.

An alternative that is gaining in popularity is school visit programs. If you and your dog enjoy interacting with young people, consider combining entertainment with some education. You could have a major impact on the dog owners of the future by demonstrating the basics of training and acquainting them with a well-socialized dog: yours. Speak with the staff or teachers at your local school system if this idea interests you. If your dog enjoys lying around in the company of kids, the Reading with Rover program may be right for you. Kids just learning to read find that dogs provide wonderfully nonjudgmental ears.

You can also check out talent competitions. At county or state fairs, pet walks, pet superstores, even on the Internet, you can compete against other dog owners just as convinced that their dog is the most talented canine on the face of the planet. Prizes can range from dog bowls and leashes to cash and a year's supply of dog food. Judges are most likely to be impressed by an act rather than a few disjointed tricks. You can either chain behaviors to tell a story, or work up a routine where you provide the flash and patter to connect your dog's talents together. It's even more impressive if you can work at some distance from your dog. But know your limits—mistakes will count against you unless you are mentally agile enough to cover them.

If you'd rather entertain than compete, you can hit the party circuit. Be the star attraction at your own gathering or offer to put on a show at your friends'.

The big attraction among the nonprofessional set is theater. High school, college, and local theater groups sometimes need dogs for their productions. *Annie*, *The Wizard of Oz*, and *Peter Pan* are the best-known of the plays with major canine roles. If your dog has the look to suit the play, so much the better, but having a trained dog may prove more important than mere appearance.

To work in theater, you definitely need to be able to direct your dog from a distance. You will have to remain hidden in the wings while your canine thespian takes his turn on the boards.

. . . AND FORTUNE

Before dollar signs start dancing before your eyes, you need to be aware of a little regulation. The United States Department of Agriculture (USDA) oversees any and all performing animals. To be paid for your services—even to appear in local theater without being paid—you must be licensed.

But there is another way. Contact any animal training agencies in your area. You can locate them in the Yellow Pages or by contacting your film commission or by reading film industry publications. In the Los Angeles area, the largest publication is the *LA411*. *The Creative Handbook* North American edition covers the entire United States and Canada. Both of these publications also list all of the film commissions in the United States. Working under the auspices of an agency, you will be licensed under their USDA agreement and covered by their insurance (otherwise difficult to obtain).

Before you contact an animal training agency, you and your dog should be ready. Your dog must be well behaved with people, and it is very helpful if he is also socialized to other dogs and other animals such as cats and horses. He must have at least basic obedience training, and advanced obedience is preferred. Experience with acting behaviors is a definite plus.

When you approach an animal training agency, keep in mind that not all of them are receptive to the idea of working with outside dogs. Some companies may keep 50 or 75 of their own dogs and work only with them. But others may need a stable of outside talent to meet the demands of different jobs. If an agency is open to the idea of using outside talent, the first thing they will probably do is ask you to send pictures of your dog.

You do not have to go out and have professional studio shots made of your dog. Normal $3^1/_2 \times 5$ or 4×6 photographs will be fine as long as they follow some basic guidelines. The photograph should show only your dog, in a sit and/or a stand position, with the dog filling most of the space. Try sending several of the same shot, plus a few shots of any special behaviors the dog does. If you have a pooch who excels at something like leaping high into the air to catch a Frisbee, a good action shot could be included. Enclose information along with the pictures. The agency will be interested in your dog's height, weight, age, and any training, as well as what other creatures your dog gets along with.

A company that likes your photos will probably then ask to see you and your dog. Bring some more photographs along, in case the agency decides to represent you. Some companies may offer dog training classes geared toward teaching behaviors that are used in the film and print industries. Others may suggest some training courses you should take.

If you do get a company interested, they may ask for an exclusive agreement. You will have to decide if this is acceptable. If it's the only agency in the county, you should probably just go ahead and sign. But if there is competition in your area, you may want to better your odds by being represented by as many companies as possible. See if this may be agreeable. Should you have the good fortune to be signed on by more than one agency, be sure to ask them to call you if the prospect of a job for your dog comes up. That way you can be sure that you won't have two companies sending out the same dog's picture for one job.

If you have gotten this far, you are very fortunate. If you actually land a job, you have bested all the odds. If fortune should smile on you, matters will now proceed as follows.

For a large job, there may be some pretraining involved, specific things that your dog will have to learn to fill the bill. This is ideal. You and the professional trainer can get to know each other, and more important, your dog can get to know the professional trainer.

You want your dog to be comfortable with the trainer because odds are that when it comes time to go on location, you won't be invited along. The trainer wants the dog's undivided attention, and your presence will probably be deemed distracting. If you have had the opportunity to watch the trainer work with your dog, and have become comfortable with the person yourself, this shouldn't be a problem. Many dogs perform better for the professional trainer, and the production company is paying for a professional to work the dog, after all.

If you are invited along (and it's up to the trainer to decide), take your cues from the trainer. There is a lot to know about being on a set. Stay out of the way. Do not, repeat, do not ask for autographs or take photographs. Never get in the way of any production people or talk while they are rolling sound. These people are professionals at their jobs and the best thing you can do is attempt to be invisible.

Should you be on the scene while your dog is being worked, it is important to remember that you got into this because it's fun. If you get stressed, you are going to pass that along to your dog. Relax, let the pros do their thing, and remember to have fun.

Most people think of performing opportunities only in movies and television, or maybe theater, but there are actually more opportunities in other areas. The print media is a huge market and includes greeting cards, calendars, T-shirts, puzzles, and print advertising. Advertising media itself covers print, in all its various forms, and television. Most businesses are well aware that animals in ads really attract attention. Corporate videos sometimes use animals, as do fashion shows.

If you just can't find an agency within a few hundred miles of where you live and you really want to get involved in performance work yourself, we can't say that your odds are good. But here are some suggestions to help you on your way.

Being able to train your dog is, of course, important. He will need to be well versed in obedience and in industry behaviors such as *Hit a mark*, *Speak*, and *Wave*. But knowing how best to handle the dog when you're actually on the scene is even more crucial. The animal's safety comes first (and never forget this in the excitement of the moment), but the next most important item is getting the shot. Work your dog in every possible location and situation so that you'll both be ready for anything.

You need to obtain an Exhibitors License from the USDA. There are two regional offices (see the end of the book). You will be subject to annual inspections, and there will be regulations covering kennels, tags on your dogs, and a variety of other issues.

For anyone to know that you are in the business, you will need to get yourself listed with your local or state film commission and advertise in a film industry publication. The two mentioned previously (with contact info at the end of the book), the *LA411* and *The Creative Handbook,* are good choices, but their rates are fairly high.

You will have to obtain liability insurance. This may be your most difficult task, and even more expensive than the advertising.

You will need to have a service contract drawn up, and to familiarize yourself with how to set and quote daily rates, pretraining rates, and all sorts of other expenses.

Taking television, stage, or film courses will help you understand what to expect. It won't prepare you for the adrenaline rush of your first professional appearance on a set, but at least you'll have some experience.

There are some definite "rules of the road" if you are representing yourself on a set, and these apply whether the set is for a high-budget movie or a very low-budget photo shoot.

Be on time. In fact, be early if possible. It may give you a chance to rehearse on location without being in anyone's way. Then be prepared to wait.

Be prepared to do far more than you were told. The rule is that the job is never exactly as advertised. A job that on the phone was "the dog just has to sit and look at the actor" may become "have the dog come into the room, look around, lie down, sit back up, stare at the actor, bark, and run out of the room." You are expected to deliver whatever is requested.

Stay out of the way. Check in with your contact (usually the assistant director if you've reached the big time). Then don't ask questions of anyone, and don't answer them either. Discussing fees or how you just happened to fall into this job will not endear you to anyone. Be quiet and observe.

Keep your dog in your vehicle or in a crate out of the way. Otherwise you will constantly be telling people not to pet the dog. You're there to work, after all. You want to look like pros. And you want your dog's attention on you, not the grip who slipped him a corned beef sandwich from the catering truck.

Pack an equipment bag of any items you might need and carry it with you. Emblazon it with your business name. Be sure to include water for your dog.

Above all else, be safe and have fun. You almost certainly got into this because you enjoyed working with your dog. Don't lose sight of that fact.

CHAPTER 4
THE BASICS

If you and your dog have already learned basic obedience, feel free to skip this chapter. You should have *Sit*, *Down*, *Stand*, and *Stay* well under control.

If you have not yet taught your dog basic obedience, it's never too late. Though we touch on teaching some obedience commands, attending a good class or taking lessons from a private trainer will accelerate your training. A good obedience foundation will allow you to get greater distance and better acting performance from your dog. It will also include the recall, or *Come*, command, which we do not use here because it doesn't apply to any of the acting behaviors we will be covering.

Animal acting is a lot of fun, but basic obedience is absolutely essential. It may, in fact, save your dog's life someday. Obedience training is a necessity in our often hazardous world. Even if you never intend to compete in the formal obedience ring, or do anything more than show off your tricks to family and friends, you shouldn't neglect your dog's basic lessons.

Though it is called "obedience" and firm control is necessary, it can still be fun!

Touche, Jack Russell Terrier

SIT

Prerequisites: None

Uses: Keeps the dog out from underfoot while you are preparing dinner, prevents him from bolting through doors, puts him in a handy position for cleaning ears or brushing teeth. Serves as the basis for a wide variety of acting behaviors. The most basic of taught behaviors, capable of being learned by a six-week-old puppy.

Action: Stand in front of or beside your dog. Hold a treat right in front of your dog's nose, then move it slightly back over the dog's head. The dog should follow the treat, raising his nose and lowering his bottom to the ground. At first, reward as soon as you have the *Sit*. Start saying "Sit" just before you show the treat. As the *Sit* becomes more reliable, wait a little while before giving the reward. You want to use the *Sit* as the starting position for some of the acting behaviors, so you want the dog to stay in a *Sit* until told otherwise. As you practice, lengthen the time the dog stays, and remember to use your release word.

If the dog doesn't respond to the food lure or continually gets up from the *Sit*, then place the dog in position. With one hand pushing down on the pressure points at either side of the dog's back just ahead of the hip bones and the other pulling up on the leash, rock the dog back into a *Sit*. Remember the same sequence applies: command ("Sit"), action (dog sits), reward (treat and praise).

Timing: Be sure to give the treat while the dog's bottom is on the ground, not after he has gotten up.

Command: "Sit"

Signal: Hold your hand flat, palm up, and raise it from a position extended at your side to approximately level with your waist. Do not raise it so fast or so high that your dog doesn't see it.

Problems: If your dog tries to jump up after the treat, you are probably holding it too high over the dog's head. The motion is more straight back over the dog than up.

Some breeds, Doberman Pinschers, for example, are known for never actually putting their butt on the ground when sitting, squatting on their haunches instead. This is an acceptable variation if it is normal for your dog.

1. With the dog in a standing position, give the command "Sit" and draw the treat back over the dog's nose until the dog sits. Reward.

OR

2. With one hand on the leash and one hand on the pressure point, rock the dog up and back into the Sit position.

3. Once the dog is in Sit position, remember to praise.

Sky the Australian Shepherd demonstrates the Sit.

DOWN

Prerequisites: *Sit*

Uses: Excellent for use as a control when you need to curb the boisterous eagerness of young dogs. The most comfortable position to use if you want the dog to stay in one place for more than a minute or so. Also serves as the basis for a variety of acting behaviors.

Action: Put the dog in a *Sit*. Hold the treat in front of the dog's nose and move it to the ground. Some dogs will lie down immediately. Quick, reward! Others will just lower their heads or slouch without quite lying down. Pull the treat slightly away from the dog along the floor to see if this will bring the dog down. If your dog is easily frustrated, reward some of her less-than-complete *Downs* to keep her interested.

If the dog doesn't respond to the food lure or continually gets up from the *Down*, place the dog in position. With one thumb on the pressure point between the dog's shoulder blades, push down and to one side or the other while pulling down on the leash with your other hand.

Timing: While the dog is learning, you can reward intermediate positions between the *Sit* and the *Down*—slouching but not actually lying down, for example. But demand a more and more correct position until you are rewarding only a full *Down*.

Command: "Down" is commonly used, but many people use this word unthinkingly when they want the dog off something rather than lying down. Cue words should mean only one thing, so if you have this problem, popular alternatives are "Crash," "Drop," "Lie" (as in "lie down"), or the German "Platz."

Signal: With your palm flat and facing the dog, swing your arm downward from chest level to waist level.

Problems: Dogs are often resistant to this behavior. If you have problems, definitely reward some early approximations of the behavior, such as the dog dipping her head or moving one leg forward. If the dog moves forward rather than lies down, change how you are moving the treat to the ground—you are probably drawing it away from the dog too much. You can also try luring the dog under an object low enough to force him to lie down to get under it and get the treat.

1. With the dog in a Sit, hold the treat in front of the dog's nose and move it to the ground, giving the command "Down."

2. Quickly reward when the dog is in the Down position.

OR

3. While pulling down on the leash, gently use the pressure point to place the dog into the Down position.

4. Quickly give the command and praise the dog when she's in the Down position.

Sky the Australian Shepherd demonstrates the Down.

STAND

Prerequisites: *Sit* is helpful

Uses: A really helpful command when grooming or examining your dog. An essential talent for any dog being shown in the conformation ring, where the dog must not only stand, but stand with each foot in correct position. Your veterinarian will also appreciate a dog that stands for a check-up.

Action: With the dog in a *Sit*, place yourself facing the dog's shoulder or ear. Hold a treat in front of the dog's nose and move it forward, directly away from the dog. If the dog follows the treat, he will automatically rise out of the *Sit*. Give the treat when he stands up.

If the dog doesn't follow the treat, have a leash to give a gentle tug forward and use your foot to gently nudge the dog in the belly just in front of the hind legs as you offer the treat. This will provide an added incentive to *Stand*.

Once you are getting a reliable performance, move to other positions around the dog, particularly standing in front of him, and work on being able to move farther away from the dog.

Timing: Be sure to give the treat while the dog is standing, preferably without a lot of fidgeting.

Command: "Stand." In the conformation ring this may be "Stack," meaning a *Stand* in a particular pose.

Signal: Draw your hand back away from the dog. If you used your foot in training, use it as part of your signal.

Problems: If the dog jumps up rather than just stands, you are holding the treat too high.

Many dogs move toward you once they're standing. Work on your *Stay* or use *Back up* (in Chapter 11) to reposition the dog.

You can also try using your lure differently. Instead of luring the dog forward with the treat, show the dog the treat and then lower it to the dog's chest and push it into his chest slightly. Some dogs will pop their back end up without moving from the place they were sitting in. If this works for you, it can help prevent the dog from moving forward.

If you use your *Stay* command, always remember to use your release cue once you're finished with the behavior.

1. With the dog in the Sit position, lure the dog forward with the treat and give the command "Stand."

2. When the dog is in the Stand position, quickly reward her.

OR

3. With the treat and leash in the same hand, gently pull forward and touch the dog's belly with your foot, give the command "Stand," and praise.

Sky the Australian Shepherd demonstrates the Stand.

STAY

Prerequisites: Any of the position commands—*Sit, Down, Stand*

Uses: Excellent for keeping the dog out of the way for brief periods, such as while you answer the door, stir the spaghetti sauce, or whatever. Necessary for gaining distance with commands—that is, put the dog in a *Sit*, tell her to *Stay*, and move a number of feet away before asking her to *Wave* or *Speak*.

Action: Put the dog in the position you wish to use. (*Down* is the most comfortable position for the dog and hardest to move from, thus easiest for the *Stay*. *Stand* is the trickiest.) Give your command and signal, move slightly away, return and reward and release. Gradually move farther away and wait longer before returning, or don't return but instead toss a treat to the dog as you release her. Remember to let the dog relax between *Stays*, and to use different positions.

Vital Information: A dog MUST be released from a *Stay*. The command means the dog is not to leave the position until given further commands or released. Never put your dog in a *Stay* and walk away and forget about her.

Timing: Do not show the dog the treat until you are ready to release her from the position. It may induce her to move. Give the treat while the dog is still in the desired position, but as you are about to release her.

Command: "Stay." (For release, "Take a break," "Free," or "Release" are often used.)

Signal: If you are near the dog, sweep your open hand directly toward the dog, stopping just short of touching her nose with your palm. At a distance, hold your hand up palm outward, like a traffic cop ordering someone to stop.

Problems: The dog breaks the *Stay*. You're moving too fast and asking too much. If your hyperactive pooch can hold still for only two seconds, then ask for only two seconds and work for quite a while before extending it to three. If the dog continues to break the *Stay*, place the dog back in position each time she gets up. *Stay* is combined with any of the positions to mean the dog will remain in one place in the chosen position until given a further command or released: "Sit Stay," "Down Stay," or "Stand Stay."

Bug the Mixed Breed demonstrates the Stay.

CHAPTER 5
JUST SITTIN' AROUND

Working with the dog in a *Sit* position gives you control. You can place yourself in the best spot for interacting with your dog and not have to worry about a lot of moving around. The dog feels relatively secure and can concentrate on the work you're trying to do.

Dogs who have practiced a variety of behaviors from the *Sit* position are more likely to keep their focus on you to see if you are going to ask them to do something besides just sit there. This can certainly work to your advantage in the obedience ring. But beware—dogs can also become quite the innovators, throwing behaviors at you to see if they might get rewarded. If you want to remain in control, reward trained behaviors only when you have asked for them . . . not when the dog decides to throw them at you, no matter how cute it may be.

Therapy dogs win over patients and staff just by the simple act of kissing patients or waving goodbye.

Conformation dogs don't sit when in the show ring, of course. But the muscle tone in their lower backs and thighs will be improved by sitting up. And doing a little showing off while the judge is busy with other dogs (without disrupting the class) can get the crowd on your side.

For actual acting work, *Wave*, *Sit up*, *Play dead*, and *Where's your nose?* are requested behaviors. And they have excellent potential for storytelling. (See Chapter 12 for suggestions.)

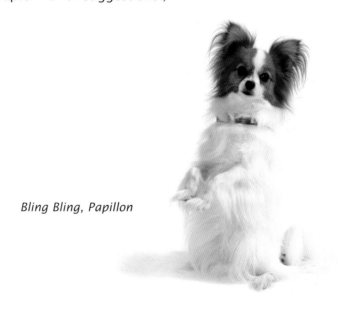

Bling Bling, Papillon

WAVE/HIGH FIVE

Prerequisites: *Sit, Stay*

Uses: A good "story" behavior, useful for weaving into a sequence of events. Can cheer the home team with a *High five* or *Wave* at departing guests. A really strong *Wave* or *High five* can improve reach in the front legs. Alternating left and right legs in quick succession gives some quick aerobic exercise. Once *Wave* is taught, you can also perform it from a *Stand* position, converting it into a high kick much loved in the sport of canine freestyle.

Action: Stand in front of your dog. Put the dog in a *Sit*. Hold a treat in your closed hand. Hold the treat near the dog's chest and encourage the dog to get the treat (while staying in a *Sit*). Encourage the dog with "Get it" but also command "Wave." You will be saying something like, "Get it, wave, get it, wave." Once the dog knows the behavior, you will simply command "Wave."

        When a front paw comes off the ground, reward the dog with the treat. Be ready to reward for any movement of a front paw. You may get a full paw swipe at your hand right from the beginning, or you could just get a tiny, tentative lift of a foot. As you practice, try to reward a little better performance each time. Some dogs will try a lot of nuzzling, barking, and just sitting and staring. Be patient.

        Once you are getting a reliable performance, stand up. For *Wave*, toss the treat as you gradually increase your distance from the dog. For *High five*, bend over only enough for the dog to be able to reach your outstretched hand.

Timing: Be sure to give the treat while the dog's paw is in the air or pawing at your hand. When your dog understands the command, withholding the treat will get the dog to repeat the action, thus creating an active *Wave*.

Command: "Wave" or "High five"

Signal: For *Wave*, hold your hand flat and wave it at the dog. For *High five*, flatten your hand and extend it toward the dog. Your dog should perform these behaviors with either of his front feet. A signal with your right hand means the dog uses his left paw. Left hand means right paw. Lean your own body to encourage the dog to shift his weight onto the foot that will not be raised.

Problems: If the dog gets up, place him back in a *Sit*. Some dogs don't use their paws very much and will not paw at your hand. With these dogs, you can use manipulation, picking the paw up as you give your command. When they are used to this action, they should start raising their paw as you reach toward them. You can then pull your hand back to get them to extend their leg. This method will take longer and won't result in a high flashy wave. You might want to call it "Shake."

1. With the dog in the Sit position, hide a treat in your hand. Hold it down low.

2. Encourage the dog to "Get it" and give the command "Wave." Reward the dog when his foot comes off the ground.

3. When the dog starts touching your hand with his paw, stand up and start moving farther away each time.

4. Once the dog is doing well, stand far enough away so the dog can't touch you. Give the signal, command, and toss the treat to the dog.

Dudley the Labrador Retriever demonstrating a Wave.

SIT UP/BEG

Prerequisites: *Sit*, *Stay*, possibly *Wave* for big dogs

Uses: A "cute" behavior, good for eliciting giggles and "ahs" from viewers. Also excellent for improving balance and strengthening the muscles in the thighs and on either side of the lower back. A dog who wobbles when attempting this probably lacks good muscle tone in these areas. Other behaviors, such as waving or balancing a biscuit on the bridge of the nose, can be combined with *Sit up* to good effect.

Action: Stand in front of your dog. Put the dog in a *Sit*. Now pinch a treat between your fingers so it is hard for the dog to get it. Hold it right in front of the dog's nose and then move your hand upward slightly. When the dog's front feet come off the ground, give the treat while saying "Sit up." As you practice, try to reward a little better performance each time.

You can help bigger dogs along by helping them rear themselves up at first. Ask for a *Wave* and put your hand under the toes of their raised foot so they can lean on you ever so slightly, then push them up into the *Sit up* position. It's harder for the big guys to balance, and this helps them find their balance point.

When the dog sits all the way up, say "Stay" and have him balance there a moment before giving the treat and releasing. Once you are getting a reliable performance, gradually increase your distance from the dog. Toss the treat to the dog. Your aim must be excellent to avoid knocking the dog off balance.

Timing: Be sure to give the treat when the dog's front feet are off the ground, not when they have come back down. If you reward only once the dog's feet are back on the ground, he will think that the action you are after is to rear up and then come down.

Command: "Sit up"; "Beg"; "Sit pretty"

Signal: Hold both hands partially closed (as if they might be holding a treat) and move them out from your body to an extended arm position, toward the dog.

Problems: If the dog rises up off his haunches, you are holding the treat too high. Keep it right on the dog's nose.

If the dog has trouble holding the position, practice with him sitting in the corner to help his balance and control. Or use the large-dog technique of helping him balance by letting one foot rest on your hand. Don't get discouraged—this behavior is a real crowd-pleaser.

1. Pinching the treat between your fingers, draw it directly over the dog's nose.

2. When the dog's feet come off the ground, give the treat while saying the command "Sit up."

3. Using hand signals, give the command "Sit up, Stay." Then toss the treat to the dog while she is sitting up.

4. For big dogs, it can help to let the dog rest one foot on your hand while training.

Bobby the Mixed Breed demonstrates Sit up.

Bling Bling the Papillon demonstrates Sit up.

BANG/PLAY DEAD

Prerequisites: *Sit, Down, On Your Side, Head Down*

Uses: People love to "shoot" their dogs. Also good as part of a storytelling chain of behaviors. Especially impressive with the dog facing away from the shooter. A nice variation on "puppy push-ups"—instead of alternating *Sit* and *Down*, use *Sit* and *Bang*.

Action: Put the dog in a *Sit* and stand close in front of her. Say "Bang down" and give your signal for *Down*. When the dog is down, say "Bang on your side" and give your signal for this. If the dog keeps her head up to look at you, say "Bang head down." When the dog is flat out on her side, tell her to stay. Give the treat as you give her your release word.

 After you have practiced and your dog seems to be getting it, phase out all the extra commands and just use a single command ("Bang") or use body language to help her. Practice at odd moments, not just when you are working a full session with your dog.

Timing: Try to offer the treat while the dog is still on her side. Many dogs will straighten up to eat, however.

Command: "Bang"

Signal: Form your hand into a gun, point it at the dog, and shoot.

Problems: "Dead" dogs often have wagging tails. Try frowning at the dog to see if that will stop it. Or leave it alone, knowing that people will laugh at the liveliness of your "dead" dog.

 If your dog is not responding, you will need to work on *On your side* (page 36) more, and help the dog by placing her in position. If she responds slowly, make a bigger deal about her getting into position and be faster with the reward.

 If, in front of an audience, you give the command and the dog doesn't respond, cover up by saying, "Drat! Missed!" and shoot her again. If the dog goes down but doesn't die all the way, say, "Only winged her" and shoot again.

1. With the dog in a Sit, point your finger gun at the dog, give the command "Bang down" and give your signal for Down.

2. When the dog is down, say "Bang on your side" and give your signal for On your side.

3. Practice taking out the extra commands, just using the word "Bang" and your body language.

4. Stand up and practice working from different positions.

Ricochet the Dalmatian demonstrating Play dead.

WHERE'S YOUR NOSE?

Prerequisites: *Sit, Stay; High Five/Wave* is helpful

Uses: Good for storytelling performances, such as asking the dog to be sure his nose is ready before having him search for something. Also the basis for a more advanced trick, *Hide your eyes*, in which the dog lies down and covers his eyes with both paws.

Action: You will need a prop to help you—a bobby pin, hair scrunchie, or cloth tape. One in particular may work better with your dog. Put the prop on the dog's muzzle clipped to some hair or the whiskers at the side of the muzzle on your dog's dominant side (Is your dog left- or right-pawed?) or put the scrunchie on his muzzle. When the dog paws at his nose, give the command "Where's your nose?," take off the prop you are using, and give a treat.

Timing: There is a lot for you to do here. The quicker you can remove whatever device you are using and offer a treat, the stronger the association the dog will make with swiping his paw over his nose. If you are inclined to try clicker training this would be a good place to use it, as you could mark the behavior while it is still occurring and then remove the prop and deliver the treat.

Some dogs are capable of staying in this position. Give the command *Stay* while the dog's paw is on his nose for a more impressive performance. (Remember to use your release.)

Command: "Where's your nose?" if the dog can stay, or "Wipe your face" if the dog just paws at his nose

Signal: Wipe your own flattened hand down your own nose.

Problems: Some dogs are very stoic and will simply sit there with the prop on their nose. Try different items to see if another gets more response. Ponytail scrunchies often work well because they are large and block the dog's vision. If you have not already taught the *High five/Wave*, go back and do that—it may give your dog the idea to use his paw. You can also try blowing on the prop or in the dog's ear, but be careful—some dogs tend to snap when you do this. Touching the object with your finger can also make the dog more aware of the prop.

1. With the dog in a Sit, place your prop on the dog's muzzle.

2. Encourage the dog to wipe the prop and give your command and signal.

3. When the dog wipes the prop, reward the dog and remove the prop.

4. Once you're no longer using the prop, ask for a better performance each time and try to get the dog to stay in the position.

Ruby the Australian Cattle Dog demonstrates Where's your nose?

CHAPTER 6
DOWN IN FRONT

Down is usually the most difficult position to teach, but once it is learned, it is pretty secure. A dog in a *Down* will tend to stay in a *Down*. So it is a good position for working on further behaviors. Dogs seem to find the "tricks" in this chapter pretty easy stuff. If you want some quick success, try these.

Though these behaviors may be relatively easy to teach, they can be quite impressive. If you want your dog to look ashamed or depressed on cue, practice *Head down*. Then you could have him *Crawl* to you for forgiveness. *Roll over* is always a big favorite at pet therapy sessions, and can even be helpful in grooming if you allow your dog to lie down while being brushed. *On your side* is rarely used on its own, but is the foundation for other behaviors such as *Bang, you're dead* and *Roll over*.

Crawling is excellent indoor exercise for dogs. It works on the shoulders, spine, neck, and hindquarters. (You should, of course, be sure your dog has no physical problems in these areas before you ask him to perform.) Be very sure that your dog understands he will be rewarded for these behaviors only when you ask for them.

In this chapter we will offer some physical manipulation choices. It's difficult to get a really good *Head down* without a little physical assist. A dog just learning *Roll over* may need a helpful nudge to get all the way over. *On your side* can be lured, but you might have to help the dog into position. If you had problems with *Down*, you may encounter some resistance here. Dominant dogs do not simply accept being pushed into position. But patience and enticing treats should get you through. If you have *real* problems—if the dog growls when you try to guide him into position—you need to work on more important matters than tricks. But as long as you have a solid relationship with your dog, it will be to both of your advantages for him to learn to accept handling.

Bobby, Mixed Breed

HEAD DOWN/HEAD UP

Prerequisites: *Down*

Uses: This is an acting behavior. A dog with his chin on the floor, eyes rolled up to watch you, can't help but look sad or ashamed. You provide the appropriate commentary, such as, "I caught you stealing that cookie from the cookie jar. Now what do you do? That's right, look ashamed." If you use this behavior to its best advantage, you can get some great crowd response.

Action: Put the dog in a *Down*. Crouch or kneel beside her. With one hand, hold your treat on the floor a couple of feet in front of the dog. With the other hand across the dog's neck directly behind the ears, gently push the dog's head down so that her chin is on the floor between her front paws. Give your command, hold her head there for a second or two, then give a treat, your release cue, and praise as you let go. (It's nearly impossible to give the dog a treat while in the *Head down* position.) When your dog seems to understand your request, use your *Stay* command and remove your hands. Have the dog hold the *Head down* for a couple of seconds before giving the treat and releasing.

For *Head up*, do a *Head down* and hold the treat in front of the dog's nose, but then move the treat up. The dog's head should follow. Always do more *Head down* than *Head up*, and give the treat at different times. That way, the dog will offer both behaviors equally well, not knowing when the treat will be offered.

Timing: Give the treat while the dog's chin is on the ground, then release quickly because the dog will usually pick her head up to chew.

Command: "Head down"; "Head up"

Signal: Be sure your signals here are obviously different from your *Down* and *Sit* signals. Point to the floor for *Head down*. Keep your hand in the same shape and move it up, index finger pointing toward the dog, for *Head up*.

Problems: Some dogs have a habit of turning their head to one side or the other so it rests on a paw rather than the floor. While you are in the learning phase of this behavior, position the dog so her chin is on the floor between her paws. It is visually more effective, and if you want to later teach *Hide your eyes*, you need the dog's paws free.

For a dog who resists this behavior, it's important that she is rewarded the second her chin touches the floor. Don't hold her there if she is struggling. Place her in position, give the command, have her head touch the floor, and reward. She will eventually stop fighting as she gets used to this. Then start telling her to stay for a gradually longer performance of the behavior.

1. With the dog in a Down, place one hand on the pressure point behind the head and with the other hand hold the treat on the floor.

2. Push gently down on the dog's head while giving the command "Head down." Try to hold her there for a few seconds before giving the treat.

3. Once the dog is doing well, stop placing the dog into position. Just give the signal and the command and toss the treat to the dog.

Matilda the Basset Hound demonstrates Head down.

ON YOUR SIDE/STRAIGHTEN UP/OTHER SIDE

Prerequisites: *Down*

Uses: This behavior serves mainly as the basis for other behaviors. Both *Roll over* and *Bang, you're dead* require *On your side* as a foundation. It's also useful in making large dogs seem less intimidating in pet therapy work or school programs. A dog lying flat out and showing his tummy is pretty nonthreatening, especially if his tail is thumping at the same time. It can also be part of doggy aerobics—alternate *Sit*, *Down*, *On your side*, *Straighten up*, *Other side*, *Sit*.

Action: Put your dog in a *Down* and kneel down to one side. Look at the dog's hips. If they are shifted to one side, you will roll him toward the leg that's tucked under him. Hold a treat and move it over the dog's shoulder that is going to face up once the dog is on his side. The dog will have to twist his neck to follow the treat, and this will naturally cause his body to shift onto one side. (See first photo for *Roll Over*, page 43.) Say your command ("On your side") and give the treat to flatten the dog out as much as possible.

If this isn't working for you, try using some physical manipulation. Take the front leg on the same side as the hip that's tucked in one hand and place your hand on the dog's neck and push him gently onto his side while saying, "On your side." Give a treat when he's flat on the floor.

Shift your weight back to the center and encourage the dog to come back to a normal down position while saying "Straighten up." Repeat the behavior going in the other direction. (Use a lure to get the dog to shift his weight onto the opposite hip if he doesn't do it himself.)

Timing: Give your treat while the dog is flat on his side and quickly give your release word, as many dogs will straighten up to eat. Use your *Stay* command to keep him on his side for a few seconds before giving the treat and releasing.

Command: "On your side"; "Straighten up"; "Other side"

Signal: Flatten both hands and extend them away from your body and flop them in the same motion you used to place the dog in the position. Shifting your body helps cue the dog in the direction you want him to go. For *Straighten up*, bring your hands back to the starting position.

Problems: All animals favor one side over the other. Figure out your dog's better side and use that for the initial learning period. Probably the most difficult part of this behavior is getting the dog to shift his hips to go in the other direction.

If you find yourself wrestling with your dog, and your dog is winning, stop. Try using your most enticing treat to lure him into position.

1. With the dog in a Down, place one hand on his neck and hold the dog's outside leg. Notice that the trainer is rolling the dog toward the tucked-under hip.

2. Gently push the dog onto his side while giving the command "On your side." Reward the dog.

3. Now shift your weight back to the center and encourage the dog to come up to the normal down position while saying "Straighten up." Reward.

4. Once your dog is doing well, stop placing your dog into position. Give the signal and the command and reward your dog.

Zane the Weimaraner demonstrating On your side.

CRAWL

Prerequisites: *Down*

Uses: Actually required for the "crawl tunnel" obstacle in UKC agility. Useful for search and rescue work. Regularly seen in commercial and TV or movie acting work. Surprisingly effective at building up shoulders, hindquarters, and the spinal column. Excellent for combining behaviors for storytelling, especially if you lean toward war stories or Westerns.

Action: Put the dog in a *Down*. Crouch or kneel slightly in front of and to the side of the dog. Hold a treat in whichever hand is more in front of the dog, with the other hand slightly above the dog's shoulders. Entice the dog forward to get the treat. If the dog starts to get up, use your other hand to exert enough pressure to keep the dog down. Don't hold your hand on the dog, just push and release.

Don't ask for a lot at first. Your dog may have to build up some muscles to be good at this. Try to stay calm and low-key, as your dog is more apt to stay down while moving slowly.

Timing: Be sure the dog is in a *Down* when you give the treat.

Command: "Crawl"

Signal: Hang both your hands down toward the floor and wiggle your fingers enticingly.

Problems: Some dogs, presumably those with weak shoulders, will keep their front end on the ground but lift their rears up and move in an odd sort of crouch. Gently tap the dog's butt down and ask for only very short distances at first. Also keep the dog moving slowly, as this helps to keep the dog down. Check with your veterinarian if your dog really seems to have trouble with this behavior. Anatomical problems such as hip dysplasia can make it very uncomfortable for a dog to *Crawl*.

1. With the dog in a Down, hold a treat in front of the dog and hold your other hand slightly above the dog's shoulder. Entice the dog forward to get the treat. Give the command "Crawl."

2. If the dog starts to get up, push on the dog's shoulders to keep him down and then release. Don't hold your hand on the dog's shoulders.

3. When the dog is crawling well, get in front of the dog and ask the dog to crawl to you.

Sky the Australian Shepherd demonstrates Crawl.

CROSS YOUR LEGS

Prerequisites: *Down, Wave*

Uses: Can be combined with other behaviors, such as *Head down*, to create a variety of expressive positions. If you teach both directions, can be used as an unusual rhythmic move in Freestyle. Poses a dog nicely for photographs.

Action: Teach a *Foot touch* to your hand. With your dog in a sit, extend your right hand as if you were going to shake hands with the dog. (Having taught *Wave* first will make your dog more apt to extend his paw to touch your hand.) Give a treat when he lifts his foot and makes contact. Start saying *Touch* as you extend your hand.

Now put the dog in a *Down*. Try to make sure he is positioned in a square "sphinx" *Down*, rather than rolled onto one hip or the other. This will make it easier for him to shift his front legs. Extend your hand, keeping it low, and give your *Touch* command. Reward when the dog makes contact.

Position your hand so the dog has to start to cross his leg over the other one to reach your hand to perform the *Touch*, or have him follow your hand with his foot (one may work better than the other with your dog). Start saying your "Cross 'em" cue as you extend your hand. As you practice, move your hand so your dog finishes crossing his legs, with one lying on the other.

Once you are doing well, extend your hand but take it away before the dog can actually touch it. After some practice, stand up and use your verbal cue and convert extending your hand to your signal of crossing your wrists over.

Use your other hand to teach your dog to cross his legs in the other direction, moving the opposite leg. Use a different verbal cue for each direction, or cross your wrists in opposite directions as a visual signal.

Timing: If you have trouble getting a treat to the dog while his foot is touching your hand, you may want to use a marker, either a short word ("Yes") or a clicker.

Command: "Cross 'em," "Criss cross"

Signal: Cross your arms at the wrists—one direction for left foot over right, the opposite direction for right foot over left.

Problems: Take the time to teach a strong *Foot touch* so that when you ask your dog to follow your hand with his foot, the behavior won't fall apart. If you encounter problems at this point, go back to working on a straightforward *Foot touch*.

If the dog doesn't hold the position, use your "Stay" cue and only ask for a few seconds at first. Extend the time gradually.

1. Once you have taught a Foot touch, put your dog in a Down and cue the touch.

2. Start moving your hand so that the dog has to cross his leg over to touch.

3. Have the dog's foot follow your hand without actually touching.

4. Stand up and use your cue and signal.

Bobby the Mixed Breed demonstrating Cross your legs.

ROLL OVER

Prerequisites: *Down, On Your Side*

Uses: This behavior seems to delight children for some reason, especially if you can have your dog do two or three in a row.

Action: Put the dog in a *Down* and do *On your side* to whichever side your dog favors. Now take a treat, show it to your dog, and move the treat over the dog's shoulder toward her backbone, the same as you did when teaching *On your side*. The dog should twist her neck to follow the treat. If the neck twists far enough, the body will follow. Once the body starts over, you should have the dog's feet in the air. (This position, with the dog on her back, feet in the air, belly totally exposed, is a behavior in itself.) Continue to lure her all the way over with the treat. If she doesn't complete the roll on her own, take one of the front legs and nudge it in the direction the dog is going to complete the *Roll over*.

Timing: Remember to give the command just before you start to lure the dog over and give the treat once she's all the way over but still in a *Down*. Do not let her up from the *Down* until you are ready. If you want to do more than one *Roll over* at a time once you are experienced, the dog will need to remain down.

Command: "Roll over"

Signal: Draw a circle in the air in front of you, going in whichever direction you are asking the dog to go.

Problems: If your dog doesn't follow the treat well enough to get her feet in the air, use a more enticing treat. If the dog goes halfway but then stops, try physically moving the dog the rest of the way. If your dog is ordinarily strongly food motivated but resists this behavior, suspect some physical problem and discuss it with your veterinarian.

    If your dog is fine physically but reluctant to *Roll over*, realize this is a very vulnerable position. You can gradually shape the behavior by giving a treat for any movement at first, then asking for a response closer to the behavior each time.

1. With the dog in a Down, give the command "On your side" and lure the dog's head with the treat over her shoulder toward her backbone.

2. Continue to lure the dog so that her body follows her head and give the command "Roll over."

3. Continue all the way over until the dog is back in a Down position and reward her.

T-Bone the Mixed Breed during Roll over.

4. Once the dog will Roll over, cue the dog with your signal and/or command.

T-Bone the Mixed Breed demonstrates Roll over.

CHAPTER 7
THE STAND-IN

Working from the *Stand* is less secure than working from other positions. It's just so easy for the dog to move or to go into a *Sit* or a *Down*. It's best to practice behaviors from other positions first so that you are more experienced in your actions and timing. Be sure your dog's *Stand* is solid. Then you're ready.

The following behaviors have a wide variety of uses. *Feet up*, for example, can prove helpful in everyday life. An aging 80-pound dog is more than a handful to lift up onto something, but if he puts his front feet up on the car or grooming table, it's easy to boost the rear end up.

Walk seems to delight young and old spectators alike, and is wonderful for pet therapy work. *Circle* can be good indoor exercise, especially if your dog whips herself into a frenzy when doing multiple circles. And what better way to end a performance than by taking a *Bow*? Dogs already know how to do this—you've probably seen your dog doing a play bow during play time— you're just attaching a command to it.

Most of these behaviors are more effective if there is some distance between you and your dog. For any behavior, practice until your dog is performing it reliably, then gradually edge away from the dog. If problems crop up, stay close until you've worked them out, then start increasing distance again. Anyone doing professional animal acting work is nearly always a considerable distance from their performers. Even those of us just doing it for fun find it much more impressive when handler and dog are separated.

Clever, Mixed Breed

FEET UP

Prerequisites: *Stand, Stay*

Uses: As mentioned, a variety of practical uses, particularly for large dogs. Getting up on a grooming table, exam table, or into an SUV are all easier with *Feet up*. Also wonderful for pet therapy work. Dogs can put their feet up on beds or wheelchair arms, making it easier for their admirers to reach them.

Action: Put the dog in a *Stand* facing some surface at a convenient height. Be sure the surface, whatever it is, will not tip under the dog's weight. Large footstools, dining room chairs, and flat-topped trunks work well. Hold a treat in front of the dog and move it forward above the surface you have chosen. Pat the surface. Encourage the dog to get the treat. Once you are getting the dog's feet on the surface, delay the treat for a few seconds while telling the dog to "Stay."

Timing: Give the treat while the dog's feet are solidly on the surface.

Command: "Feet up"

Signal: With both hands, point from the dog to the surface on which you want *Feet up* performed.

Problems: Some dogs interpret your patting of a surface as an invitation to jump completely onto it. Try just moving the treat slightly over the surface without any further encouragement. If the dog still jumps up, use your leash to guide him into the correct position, then praise and give the treat. Or use a narrow platform that doesn't invite jumping onto it, such as a length of 2 × 4 securely placed across a short open space.

Other dogs are extremely reluctant to put their feet up on furniture, especially if you have been firm in teaching the dog not to get on couches or chairs. Try lifting the dog's paws onto the surface the first couple of times you attempt the behavior. Or start practicing this behavior outside on picnic benches, tree stumps, or whatever is the right height for your dog.

1. With the dog in a Stand, show her the surface you want her to put her feet up on.

2. Hold a treat in front of the dog and lure her forward so that she puts her front feet on the chair, while giving the command "Feet up."

3. Once she's doing well, have her stay in that position and toss the treat to her.

Clever the Mixed Breed demonstrates Feet up.

PUT 'EM UP/WALK

Prerequisites: *Stand, Stay*

Uses: This rise out of the *Stand* position requires strength in the entire hindquarters. Standing in one place (*Put 'em up*) also calls for excellent balance. This is good foundation training for a dog that will be competing in agility. But a cute little dog walking on her hind legs is always going to steal the show.

Action: Put the dog in a *Stand* and, with a treat in one hand, draw your hands up over the dog and raise them straight up above the dog, enticing her to straighten her back legs and stand up. Reward and release. When she is doing well, hold the treat so the dog has to work at getting it from your hand while she is standing up, which will keep her in the position longer and teach her to balance. After some practice, give the command "Put 'em up, stay" and move away from the dog, rewarding by tossing the treat while she is standing up. This stationary standing up is *Put 'em up*.

Now that you have *Put 'em up* on command, you can teach the dog to walk on her hind legs by asking her to come forward while she's still in the *Put 'em up* position. Ask for just one or two steps in the beginning, then toss the treat.

Timing: Be sure to give the treat while the dog is on her hind legs, not after she has come back to a *Sit* or a normal *Stand*. When you are working on gaining distance, tossing a treat to your standing dog will be quite a test of your accuracy.

Command: "Put 'em up"; "High"; "Walk"

Signal: Hold your arm straight out as if you're pointing up high to something.

Problems: Some dogs find rising up quite difficult. You can try starting from a *Sit* to see if that helps the dog. Dogs with back or hip problems should not be asked to perform this behavior. Check with your veterinarian if you have any doubts.

If your dog has a difficult time balancing, use your most enticing treat and make it hard for the dog to get it. She will concentrate more on the treat and less on the fact that she's standing up. Don't reward the dog if she's jumping to get the treat.

1. With the dog in
a Stand, hold the
treat well above
the dog's head.

2. When the dog comes up, give the
command "Put 'em up" and try
to keep the dog standing up for
several seconds. Give the reward.

3. When the dog is doing well, move
away from the dog, command the
dog to "Put 'em up, stay," and toss
the treat to the dog.

Fly the Beagle
demonstrates Put 'em up.

TAKE A BOW

Prerequisites: *Stand*

Uses: The perfect behavior to finish any performance. It also stretches the muscles all along the spine.

Action: Put the dog in a *Stand*, put a treat in your hands, and quickly push the treat toward the dog between her front legs until her front end starts going down. Say "Bow" and give her the treat. The next step is to make sure her front legs are completely on the ground before rewarding her.

Or, if you are not in a hurry, you can experience how it feels to teach by mimicking behavior. The play bow is such a natural behavior that it is one of the easiest to teach in this way.

When your dog is in a playful mood, assume the play bow position yourself. Waggle your rear end. See if your dog will return the *Bow*. Reward any move she makes toward giving you a *Bow*. Teaching by mimicking generally takes longer than teaching by lure and/or manipulation, but there are some behaviors, such as yawn, that can be taught only this way.

Timing: Give the treat while the dog's front end is on the ground, but be sure that the back end doesn't collapse. Release the dog before she goes down.

Command: "Bow" or "Take a bow" ("Bow" can sometimes sound like "Down," and might be confusing to your dog.)

Signal: Make both hands into fists and move them down while flicking your wrists so that your hands move up.

Problems: You can use a leash looped around the dog's belly to hold up the back end if your dog keeps downing. If someone else is usually available while you are training, you can have the second person stay at the dog's side and place a hand under the dog's belly just forward of the hips in place of the leash.

1. With the dog in a Stand, quickly push the treat toward the dog between her front legs while giving the command "Bow."

2. When the dog's front legs go flat on the floor and her back end is up, reward her.

3. Once the dog is doing well, give the signal and the command and toss the treat to the dog.

Bobby the Mixed Breed demonstrates Bow.

CIRCLE LEFT/CIRCLE RIGHT

Prerequisites: *Stand*

Uses: This is a good exercise for developing suppleness in your dog, and can prove helpful for agility dogs. If you plan on teaching the more advanced *Figure eight through the legs* or *Grapevine/Weave*, some preliminary practice with circling can make it easier. There is a sport called Canine Freestyle, in which handler and dog perform a routine of their own devising to music. Circling can be very effective as part of such a routine.

Action: Put the dog in a *Stand* in front of you. Put a treat in your left hand and lead the dog in a circle clockwise by moving the treat around. If this works, practice this way, using the left hand for circling clockwise and the right hand for circling counterclockwise.

    If your dog does not follow the treat, change how you are moving it. You may be holding it too high or moving too quickly or slowly. If after some experimentation it still doesn't work, put the dog's leash in the same hand as the treat and physically lead the dog around while moving the treat in the circle. After you have done this for a while, try again with just the treat.

Timing: Give the treat just as the dog is finishing the *Circle*. Right from the beginning, vary the number of circles you ask the dog to do before rewarding it. That way the dog tends to perform better, not knowing when he's going to be rewarded.

Command: "Circle left"; "Circle right"

Signal: With your index finger pointing, draw a circle in the direction you want your dog to go. Make it more dramatic by shifting your body weight in the same direction you're pointing.

Problems: Be sure to show your dog from the beginning that more than one circle may be required to earn a treat, whether it's two or three in the same direction or a *Circle left* followed by a *Circle right*. Otherwise you may have a lot of trouble getting multiple circles later. If the dog's not circling, you may be holding the treat too high, moving too fast, or not making the circle large enough.

1. With the dog in a Stand, lure the dog around in a Circle.

2. Continue to lure the dog while giving the command "Circle left" or "Circle right."

3. Reward the dog once she has completed the Circle.

DaVinci the Greyhound during Circle.

4. Once your dog is doing well, stop luring her. Give the signal and command and toss the treat.

DaVinci the Greyhound demonstrates Circle.

CHAPTER 8
A MOVING EXPERIENCE

Now that you have some experience working on behaviors that are stationary or nearly so, it's time to try some that really move. Your control over the dog is a little looser when you start introducing movement, so you will need to be on your toes.

Go around is a natural if you happen to be working with one of the herding breeds, but any dog can do it. If you want, you can start by teaching the dog to circle around you, but then transfer the command to other objects such as a cane or a chair. You can also teach the dog to *Go around* in either direction.

Your success with *Figure eight through the legs* and the more advanced *Grapevine/Weave* will depend partially on your dog's height and the length of your legs. Great Danes and Irish Wolfhounds are not leading candidates for these behaviors. But most toy or terrier breeds are. And if you are a long-legged six-footer, there shouldn't be any problem with any of the mid-size retrievers, hounds, or others. Even if your dog's height exceeds your leg length, you can adapt this behavior by holding your leg in the air as the dog passes under.

You will need a good supply of patience and food treats for this chapter. Master these behaviors and you will have shown some real training prowess.

Fly, Beagle

GO AROUND

Prerequisites: *Stand, Sit*

Uses: Combined with the other two behaviors in this chapter, you can put on a sparkling performance where your dog performs a different behavior based on how you are standing or moving. Have the dog circle the "bad guy" in a skit to stop him from moving, then sit in front to keep a close eye on him.

Action: Stand with your feet together and your dog standing in front of you. Hold a treat in each hand. Use your right hand to lure your dog tightly around your right leg to behind you. Bring your left hand back to meet your right hand, take your right hand away, and use your left hand to continue luring the dog around you and back to the front. When you are just starting, reward during the first circle, while the dog is moving, but after a few sessions, lure the dog around twice before rewarding. Start saying your command before you start to lure. Leave the food out of your hands but make the same motion to send the dog around. Gradually reduce the motion until it becomes your signal. When the dog is moving well in as many circles as you want, have the dog sit in front of you after the final circle. If you want, you can also teach the dog to go in the other direction.

Timing: While you are training this, it's important to reward while the dog is moving. Do not add the *Sit* at the end until the dog is making multiple circles with one command.

Command: "Around," "Stop them," "Round 'em up"

Signal: With your palm flat and your arm hanging down, move your hand from in front of your right leg in a sweeping motion to your side.

Problems: If the dog doesn't follow the lure behind you, reward a few times just for a quarter of a circle, with the dog at your side. Switch to a higher-value treat. Make sure you have a good exchange of luring hands behind your back (practice without your dog if you have to).

1. Use your right hand holding a treat to lure your dog into the start of a circle around you.

2. Move the lure behind you to keep the dog moving around you.

3. Switch the hand you're luring with.

4. Continue luring around, now with your left hand.

5. Wait until your dog is completing multiple circles before asking for a Sit at the end.

Fly the Beagle being cued to Go around.

FIGURE EIGHT THROUGH THE LEGS

Prerequisites: *Stand*

Uses:
This serves as the foundation for the next behavior, the *Grapevine/Weave*. But on its own it can help boost your dog's confidence and increase flexibility. Bending is often advised to help dogs gain good jumping form, especially in agility, where dogs often have to turn sharply between jumps. Trying to perform a figure eight around your legs forces a dog to bend extensively. Be sure to practice in both directions, with the dog starting in front of you and behind you.

Action:
Stand with your legs spread a little more than shoulder width. Have the dog sit or stand behind you. Hold a treat in each hand and offer the treat with your right hand from the front between your legs while hiding the treat in your left hand. Lure your dog through your legs and around to the back of your right leg. Meet your left hand to your right hand through your legs, then hide your right hand and continue to lure the dog with your left hand through and around to the back of your left leg. Now meet your right hand to the left, hide your left hand, and continue to lure the dog through your legs. Reward—you've completed the *Figure eight*.

Once the dog shows some understanding, try to make the entire *Figure eight* in one movement. This requires dexterity on your part to switch from leading with your right hand to leading with your left. You can also try using one treat, switching it from hand to hand at the changeover point.

Once the dog is doing well, don't stop at one complete *Figure eight*—go for two, three, even four if your dog can take it. You don't want a dog who stops automatically after one pass. You can also use your legs held together and a cane as the two objects around which the *Figure eight* is performed.

Timing:
If your dog is hesitant, reward at first just for coming between your legs and gradually ask for further movement around the outside of your leg. Reward often enough to keep your dog interested and raise your sights a little at a time.

Command:
"Figure eight"; "Through the legs"

Signal:
By placing the dog and yourself in position, saying the command "Figure eight," and pointing in the direction you want the dog to go, you will cue the dog.

Problems:
If your dog will not follow the treat, change to your most enticing treat. If that still doesn't work, use your leash as a guide—pass it between your legs and hold it in your right hand so you can lead the dog through and around to the right. Or use a short traffic leash or a tab attached to the dog's collar. Hold it in the same hand as the treat and use it to guide the dog through. Be very gentle and don't ask too much at first. Your dog needs her confidence built up. Also be careful that you don't tangle yourself in the leash.

1. Standing with your legs spread a little wider than shoulder width, have your dog in a Sit behind you.

2. Hold a treat in each hand and lure the dog through your legs, keeping your other hand out of the way.

3. Continue to lure the dog back around the outside of your leg.

Richochet the Dalmatian demonstrates Figure eight through the legs.

4. When your dog gets to the back of your leg, bring your other hand through your legs to meet your lure hand.

Now pull away the first hand you were using and continue to lure the dog with your other hand.

5. Bring the dog back around the outside of your other leg.

Lure the dog as far as possible behind you, then pull away that hand and use the hand you started with to lure the dog all the way through.

6. Once the dog comes through your legs this time, she's completed the Figure eight.

Figure Eight

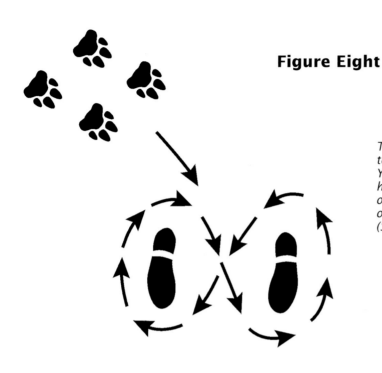

This is the path the dog will take to make a complete Figure eight. You could also start the dog heading around your right leg, or have the dog start in front of you rather than behind. (See page 58.)

Grapevine/Weave

This is the path the dog will take to perform the Grapevine/Weave. Each human footprint represents one step forward. Always remember to start your dog on the side of your back leg first so you can take a step freely without the dog being in the way. (See page 62.)

THE GRAPEVINE/WEAVE

Prerequisites: *Figure eight through the legs, Circle left/Circle right are helpful*

Uses: A good flexibility exercise. It is also closely related to the working of agility weave poles. But it is simply a charming exercise on its own. As part of your pet therapy entertainment routine, it's sure to be well received.

Action: Have the dog do a few *Figure eights through the legs* to get warmed up. Now have the dog sitting on your left side with his nose pointing toward you at a 90-degree angle to you. Have a treat in each hand. Step straight forward with your right foot, as though you're walking. Put your left hand behind your back. Lure the dog all the way through your legs with your right hand, then into a half circle so he's facing you again. Now step straight forward with your left leg. Bring your left hand behind your left leg to meet your right hand. Hide your right hand behind your back. Lure the dog all the way through your legs and into a half circle so he's facing you again. Now repeat.

Timing: Be sure to reward and praise enthusiastically the first few times your dog finds her way through your legs and back around. Don't try to take too many steps too soon or you will confuse your dog. Watch for signs of stress—this behavior can be quite confusing to the dog (and you).

Command: "Grapevine"; "Weave"; "In and out"

Signal: By placing the dog and yourself in position, giving the command "Grapevine," and pointing in the direction you want the dog to go, you will cue the dog.

Problems: Make sure you circle the dog far enough out so that when he comes back to face you he's not in the way of your moving leg. Also be sure that the dog starts on the same side as your back leg—otherwise you will kick the dog when you attempt to take a step forward. See the drawing on the previous page for the correct route.

If you are short and your dog is tall, you have a problem! If this is the case, but this behavior really appeals to you, try lifting up your leg so your dog can pass under it before you put it back down. Problems here are likely to be similar to those encountered in *Figure eight through the legs*. See that behavior for further suggestions.

1. Standing with your dog sitting facing you at your left, extend your right leg forward as if in mid-stride.

2. With the treat in your right hand, lure the dog between your legs.

3. Be sure the dog comes all the way through so your left leg is free to move.

Apple the Australian Cattle Dog demonstrating Grapevine.

4. Lure the dog around in a half circle so he's facing you from the right side.

5. Step forward with your left leg. Bring your left hand forward with its treat to meet your right hand.

6. Hide your right hand behind your back and use your left hand to lure the dog through your legs and into a half circle to face you again.

CHAPTER 9
ATHLETE TURNED ACTOR

Is your dog a bundle of energy? The following behaviors can help burn up some of that fire. Just be sure your dog is not suffering from any joint or back problems before beginning any jumping program.

All of these behaviors are variations on a theme. Try one or two or work on them all. If you have plans to compete in agility or flyball, your dog will be doing plenty of jumping anyway. These behaviors will offer a little variety.

Always start any jumping behavior at a minimal height. Increase the height gradually. And any time you change the behavior, such as working from jumping through a hoop to jumping through your arms, lower the height back to your starting position. Don't ever be in a hurry with any behavior involving jumping. Mistakes can injure your dog's body and her confidence.

Be careful of working the dog on slick floors. If you will be using jumping in your pet therapy repertoire, find an area that is carpeted or that offers secure footing for the dog. Also, if your dog is less than six months old, wait to begin your jumping training. At such a young age, the dog's bones are still growing rapidly and are more easily injured.

Gypsy, Border Collie

HOOP JUMP

Prerequisites: *Stand, Stay*

Uses: Good for maximum exercise in minimum space. Can be quite a flashy performance, especially if you have a large dog and a small hoop. Can be useful for teaching a dog to jump compactly, with feet well tucked up.

Note that you can often find inexpensive hoops in the toy department of discount stores. Some people have been lucky enough to find hoops that are made in sections, so that a section can be removed to make a smaller hoop.

Action: Position the dog in a *Stand, Stay* to your left or right. Hold the hoop slightly off the ground. Offer a treat on the side of the hoop opposite the dog and encourage the dog through. As the dog gets the idea, slowly raise the hoop. Keep raising it until you reach a height suitable for your dog's jumping efforts. You can create a more impressive show by decorating your hoop or holding it behind your back and having the dog jump back and forth through the hoop. You can cover the hoop with thin paper and have the dog rip through it. Or you can position the dog behind you, hold the hoop over your head, and crouch down to bring the hoop down to a height appropriate for your dog.

Timing: Reward the dog immediately after he clears the hoop at first. When you have raised the height, wait to reward him until the dog has collected himself after landing. As always, as your dog gains understanding of the behavior, reward intermittently.

Command: "Hoop"; "Jump"; "Through"

Signal: A sweeping arm motion in the direction the dog will be jumping.

Problems: If the dog will not go through the hoop to get the treat, try using your highest-value test. You can also try throwing one of your dog's favorite toys through the hoop. If you are having problems, reward at first just for the dog sticking his head through, then for stepping one paw through, and so on.

1. Start with the dog in a Stand, Stay. Hold the treat through the hoop.

2. Lure her through and give your command. Have her walk through at first.

3. Once she's doing well, start to raise the hoop gradually, asking for a better performance each session.

4. Remember not to move the hoop when the dog is jumping.

5. Reward the dog when she gets to the other side.

Gypsy the Border Collie demonstrates Hoop jump.

JUMP THROUGH YOUR ARMS

Prerequisites: *Hoop Jump*

Uses: Another flashy behavior that doesn't require any props once you have it trained. It does require trust both on your dog's part and on yours, because the dog will be jumping very close to your face. Some people find this far more impressive than the *Hoop jump*.

Action: Do a couple of *Hoop jumps* to warm up. Then kneel down so that the hoop is low and hold it with your arms following the curve of the hoop. At first put your arms only partway around the hoop. Hold it out as far from your body as possible. Keep your head back out of the way. Command your dog through the hoop. If she seems secure with this, move your arms more around the hoop the next time. When you have brought your arms around to form a nearly complete circle, eliminate the hoop.

Timing: Reward the dog as before, as soon as she has completed the jump.

Command: "Hoop"; "Jump"; "Through"

Signal: Forming the hoop with your arms

Problems: Many dogs are reluctant to jump close to your face, and see your arms as somehow more confining than the hoop. They may be hesitant under the new conditions you are presenting. Take your time in extending your arms around the hoop. If your dog is jumping well through the hoop and you take your time changing the look of the behavior, you should be able to work through any reluctance. If you have a training partner, he or she can help in coaxing the dog through.

1. Make sure your dog performs the Hoop jump very reliably. Now you can start wrapping your arms partway around the hoop and give the cue for the dog to jump through.

2. Still holding the hoop, start to make a smaller circle with your arms. Once the dog is doing well, you're ready to move to the next phase.

3. Now remove the hoop and have the dog jump through your arms.

Ketchup the Norwich Terrier demonstrates Jumping through your arms.

JUMP OVER LEG/BAR

Prerequisites: *Stand, Stay, Hoop Jump*

Uses: Could fit very nicely in a Canine Freestyle routine, where handler and dog perform choreography to music. Useful practice for agility, where you will encounter many bar jumps. A flashy behavior sure to impress spectators. Doesn't require any props if you are using your leg.

Action: Put the dog in a *Stand*. Start by using a bar. Hold the bar low and parallel to the ground. Entice the dog over with a treat. Gradually raise the bar. Now put the bar next to your outstretched leg and have the dog jump over it. Practice this several times, then remove the bar. Your own balance will be very important if you are doing *Jump over leg*.

Timing: Reward as before, as soon as the dog is back on the ground.

Command: "Over"; "Leg"; "Bar"

Signal: Sweep your arm over the leg or bar in the direction the dog will be jumping.

Problems: If the dog tries to go around, put your foot flat against the wall or put a chair against the wall and put your foot on it. If the dog tries to go under, you may be going too high too soon. If your dog refuses to jump at all, ask your veterinarian about physical problems.

1. Start with your dog in a Stand. Hold the treat on the other side of the bar.

2. Give the "Jump" command and have your dog jump over the bar. Reward him on the other side. Gradually move the bar higher.

3. Now that your dog is jumping the bar well, put the bar beside your leg, hold them both up together, and ask your dog to jump.

4. When your dog is accustomed to this, remove the bar and have him Jump over your leg.

Gypsy the Border Collie demonstrates Bar Jump.

ALLEY-OOP/HUG

Prerequisites: *Sit* (for small dogs), *Feet Up* (for large dogs)

Uses: With small dogs, *Alley-oop* can lead to some flashy behaviors, such as leaping from a platform across open space into the owner's arms. It can also save the owner's back when picking up the dog. For dogs too large to catch in your arms, *Feet up* can become a heartwarming *Hug*. This is not a hug you would want to use in pet therapy, as the hug recipient will be bearing some of the dog's weight.

Action: For *Alley-oop*, sit in a low chair. Using encouragement, food, or a toy tucked under your chin, encourage the dog to jump into your lap. *Be sure to catch the dog!* Pet her and love her and give her a treat—make this a positive experience before you put her down. Little by little, straighten up out of the chair. Keep your knees slightly bent to give the dog a push-off platform for getting up into your arms. Always be ready to securely catch the dog. Once she is accomplished at this, you can place her on a platform and ask her to jump to you—stay fairly close at first.

For larger dogs, you ask for a *Feet up* using your chest or shoulders as the target. Be prepared to bear the dog's weight. To make a really pretty *Hug* also have the dog do a *Head down* on your shoulder or chest. Wrap your arms around the dog to return the hug. You can even add a *Kiss* if you have taught the dog this behavior.

Timing: Be sure to make this an enjoyable behavior—the dog is putting a lot of trust in you. Don't hold a dog in the *Hug* position if she is not comfortable. Make sure you do hold a small dog comfortably and securely in your arms. Offer treats, praise, whatever will make your dog happy.

Command: "Alley-oop"; "Hug"; "Give us a hug"

Signal: Put both hands out ready to catch the dog for the *Alley-oop*. For *Hug*, bring both arms in and tap your chest or thighs.

Problems: Most problems would be caused by the handler—not catching the dog securely or stepping on the back feet of a hugging dog. Don't be concerned that teaching your dog to hug will give her license to jump up on people. This behavior, as all behaviors, should be accepted only on command.

1. While sitting down, start with the dog in a Sit in front of you.

2. Encourage the dog to jump into your lap.

3. Give the command "Alley-oop" as the dog is jumping.

Remember to catch the dog and praise and reward her.

Trouble the Mixed Breed demonstrates the end of Alley-oop.

4. Once she's jumping well onto your lap, stand partway up out of your chair, moving closer to a standing position with each session. You always need to keep your legs bent slightly to provide a platform for your dog.

5. Always hold your dog comfortably and securely when she's in your arms.

Big dogs can Hug instead of jumping into your lap. You can use Feet up with you as the target. Finnegan the Mixed Breed demonstrates.

CHAPTER 10
EXTRAS

Here are a few more behaviors, any of which could come in handy should you be lucky enough to land a professional assignment. Or they might help you win top prize in talent competitions, especially if you work on distance and minimizing your signals.

The first two of these behaviors are related, with *Counting* a more advanced form of *Speak*. If you work at it, you can make this so subtle that it truly baffles your spectators. Teaching *Whisper* makes *Say your prayers* much more effective—you don't want a dog who *shouts* his prayers, after all.

Kiss is an easy behavior to teach. Your dog probably offers plenty of this on his own. Now you're going to put it on cue. If you participate in pet therapy, you will find this a very well-received talent (though you should always ask permission before having your dog give someone a kiss).

This chapter's final behavior, *Say your prayers*, fits in quite nicely with the subject of the last chapter, putting a series of behaviors together to tell a story. If you've taught *Feet up* and *Speak*, you're close to having this behavior accomplished.

Bobby, Mixed Breed

SPEAK/WHISPER

Prerequisites: None

Uses: Part of *Say your prayers*, and the basis for *Counting*. A great behavior to have in your act; can be added to almost any storytelling routine you might devise.

Action: A lot of people teach this by waiting until the dog barks and immediately giving their command, even going so far as to set up situations that will set the dog off, such as having a friend ring the doorbell. This will eventually work, but try this if you have a good relationship with your dog and want some faster results: With the leash attached to your dog's buckle collar or harness, tie the dog to a secure object or have someone hold the leash. Stand about four to six feet out of the dog's reach and offer a treat, a ball, or whatever your dog really wants to get to. Make yourself and the object you're using really enticing. Encourage the dog to get the treat or toy. Most dogs will bark out of frustration. Any sound or any effort toward creating a sound should be rewarded. Ask for a little better performance each time. Add the command/signal to "Speak."

    To teach *Whisper*, once you have a reliable *Speak*, put your finger over your lips as if you are shushing someone and very quietly say "Speak." Continue to ask for the behavior until the dog responds with a halfhearted sort of bark. Eventually switch the word "Speak" to "Whisper."

Timing: When teaching *Speak*, as soon as the dog barks or makes any sound, throw the treat or toy to the dog. Remember, lots of praise. It probably won't take very long for your dog to catch on to this. When he seems to understand, still have him tied or held but move closer and give your command and/or signal and see if he responds to the command. If you do not get a bark, move back out to where the dog can't reach you and continue to entice him with your treat.

Command: "Speak"; "Bark"

Signal: Hold your hand up next to your head with index finger outstretched and shake it.

Problems: *Never* reward a dog for barking if you have not cued him once the behavior is taught. You do not want to create a noisy monster.

    Some dogs just do not offer a lot of barking. If you have one of these quiet types, remember in the beginning to reward any whine or snort and try to work up to a lusty bark. Or try the alternate method mentioned first under "Action."

Bobby the Mixed Breed demonstrates the Speak.

1. Have someone hold your dog on a leash or tie the leash to a secure object.

2. Entice the dog with either food, a toy, or by calling her from about four to six feet away. You may have to act goofy and maybe even play bow to your dog.

3. Continue to excite the dog until she either whines, whimpers, or speaks. Immediately reward the dog.

Keep repeating this sequence and add the command "Speak."

4. Once she performs the behavior readily, have her Sit and give the signal and command to "Speak."

COUNT/ANSWER QUESTIONS

Prerequisites: *Speak*

Uses: With some extra work, you can turn your dog into an apparent math wizard taking problems in arithmetic from the audience and having the dog answer them. Or you can do a little vaudeville turn with your dog answering stupid questions.

Action: You've taught the dog to bark on cue; now you'll teach him to stop on cue. Start by holding your hand up and giving the *Speak* cue. Have the dog bark once, lower your hand, and reward him. Now do the same thing, but hold up two fingers as you signal and have him bark twice before lowering your hand and rewarding. Do not reward him if he continues to bark after you put your hand down. Quickly giving the treat will usually stop the barking. Do the same thing for three, four, five, and so on.

Change your command to match whatever routine you are planning. Associate the word "Speak" with "How many fingers am I holding up?" until you no longer have to say "Speak." Or make the association with your silly question, such as "What did the dog say when he sat on the sandpaper?" ("Ruff," of course.)

Now you're ready for an audience. Do your vaudeville schtick, or, if you are counting, have someone pick a number between one and five or give you an arithmetic problem with an answer between one and five. Hold up the appropriate number of fingers and ask the dog, "How many fingers am I holding up?" or ask the arithmetic question and give your signal. Subtly lower your hand after your dog has reached the appropriate number of barks. Wait a beat, then reward him with a treat.

Timing: If you really want this act to be impressive, your cuing and timing are everything. Many dogs enjoy barking and will not always wait for your *Speak* signal once they know how the act works. It will help if you do not make eye contact with the dog until you are ready for his answer. A good way to get your dog to stop on cue is to learn to toss a treat with your hand at your side away from your audience so it is unobtrusive.

Command: "How many fingers am I holding up?" or "What did the dog say when he sat on the sandpaper?" or "How much is ten minus six?"

Signal: Appropriate number of fingers or body cue or facial cue. You want to work to make your cue as subtle as possible.

Problems: If your dog barks enthusiastically, make sure that you cue him at the end of your question. For instance, have him sit in front of you, but do not look at him as you say, "What did the dog say when he sat . . ." Now look at him and give your subtle cue as you finish ". . . on the sandpaper?" If your dog takes a lot of cuing, you will want to start cuing him much earlier. You need to get your timing down so that the bark comes in the correct place and your audience doesn't realize that you are cuing the dog.

After you have Speak well in hand, you can try "Whisper," using a "shush" signal.

For Counting, hold up the number of fingers you want the dog to count as your cue.

Bobby the Mixed Breed demonstrating Counting. Remember to be expressive with your body when cuing the dog.

KISS

Prerequisites: None

Uses: Wonderful for pet therapy or for dogs involved in schoolroom pet education classes. Equally useful in your everyday activities, such as when encountering children while walking in the park.

Action: You can practice this on yourself if you have to, but it is better to have helpers right from the beginning—you will want your dog to kiss anyone you indicate, not just you.

Have some meat-flavored baby food on hand. Put some of the baby food on your helper's cheek. Have the helper squat or kneel to be within easy reach of the dog. Take your dog up to the helper and say "Kiss" while maneuvering the dog toward the baby food. If the dog does not begin licking on his own, point toward the baby food and encourage him to lick it. If your dog does not seem fond of the baby food, try a different flavor or switch to peanut butter or squeeze cheese.

Make sure you are targeting the dog to the cheek with the food motivator. Some people do not like a dog kissing them on the mouth. Once the dog has licked the baby food off, have him return to you and give him a treat so he will associate kissing with getting a treat from you.

Once your dog seems to have the idea, stop walking up to the helper and stop using the baby food. Stay a little distance away and send the dog. The dog must go give a *Kiss* and return to you for his reward. Be sure to use as many different helpers as possible—men and women, young and old, tall and short.

Timing: Make sure the dog gives a couple of hearty licks before you offer any praise or a separate food reward.

Command: "Kiss"; "Go kiss"

Signal: Sweep your arm in the direction of the person while giving your command.

Problems: Shy dogs will likely have problems with this behavior, but it can also be a good confidence builder. Start with people the dog knows and accepts and make your practices short and positive. Instruct your helpers not to look at the dog and to keep still.

1. In teaching Kiss, place a small amount of whatever food reward you're using on the person's cheek.

2. Point to where the food reward is and give the command "Kiss."

3. Once the dog is doing well, stop using food on the helper's face, and just give your command "Kiss." Once the dog has kissed the person, have him return to you for the treat.

Dudley the Labrador Retriever demonstrates Kiss.

SAY YOUR PRAYERS/PRAY

Prerequisites: *Feet Up, Whisper*

Uses: A good behavior as part of storytelling. Also a nice stretching exercise for the neck and back. Both young and old spectators are likely to react with "ahs."

Action: Stand or kneel, depending on your dog's size. With your dog standing, hold your nonactive arm (your left if you're right-handed) out parallel to the ground. Have the dog do *Feet up* on the outside of your arm. Practice this for several sessions, until your dog is comfortable with it.

Now have your dog do *Feet up* on your arm, then take your treat and offer it under your extended arm to the dog, making the dog duck her head between her paws to get the treat. Give your command "Pray" and immediately reward the dog. Practice this for several sessions. Occasionally practice with the dog's feet up on a bar or an open-backed chair.

When the dog seems to be catching on, omit the *Feet up* command. Just offer your arm and give your "Pray" command. Once your dog is comfortable with this, give your command "Whisper" while your dog is in the *Pray* position. Reward. Practice this for several sessions. As your release command, say "Amen."

Timing: At first, reward the dog for each behavior you ask for—"Feet up," "Pray," "Whisper." As you become more accomplished at this, the dog has to perform the entire sequence and hold her position for several seconds before being rewarded. When you have really got it all together, the dog must actually say her prayers before being rewarded.

Command: "Say your prayers"; "Pray"

Signal: Extend your arm or point to some other chosen target as you give your command.

Problems: Dogs often take one paw off your arm as they try to tuck their head or may even jump off completely. Take it slow and be patient. You can try having your dog start from a *Sit* and see if that works better for you. Experiment with lowering or raising your arm slightly to find your dog's most comfortable position.

1. Start with the dog in a Sit with your arm extended.

2. Give your dog the command "Feet up" on your arm. Work on this for several sessions until your dog feels comfortable doing the behavior.

3. Now with the dog in the Feet up position on your arm, use a treat to lure the dog's head down through her front legs and give the command "Pray."

Bobby the Mixed Breed demonstrates Say your prayers.

CHAPTER 11
LEADING ROLES

These behaviors may be a little more difficult to accomplish, but will give you a real paw up on the competition. Many of them are quite showy on their own or can be woven into a storytelling performance.

Hit a mark and *Back up* are pretty nearly essential if you have aspirations of paid acting work. You have to be able to position your dog without getting in the way of the camera. And they can help make any performance a real crowd pleaser, by putting distance between you and your performing dog.

If you tend toward the artistic side of things, check out *Foot touch*. You can use it to have your dog play the keyboard or drums, ring a bell, or paint you an actual piece of art. You can probably find other kids' toys or instruments your dog can operate with a foot.

Hide your eyes and *Limp* can both be challenging to teach, but they're good emotional attention grabbers. Put them in your storytelling routines for a real burst of pathos.

Balance a cookie is a cute stand-alone behavior, sure to please. It's great for entertaining spectators on your pet therapy visits. You can use different sizes and shapes of treats to make the performance harder or easier.

If you accomplish the behaviors in this chapter, you're ready for more advanced work!

Diesel, Mixed Breed

HIT A MARK

Prerequisites: None

Uses: Absolutely essential in the world of animal acting, as it's used to position the dog on the set. You can use it to move your dog away from you and then ask for other behaviors at a distance, making them much more impressive. You can use multiple marks to move the dog from one spot to another.

Action: A mark can be any object the dog is comfortable standing on, so a large coffee table book or a length of 2×6 or a sandbag or a flat rock will do.

Give the command "Mark" and lure the dog to step onto the object with both front feet, then give a treat. Use your release word. After several sessions, have the dog on the opposite side of the mark from you, and step back to lure the dog toward you. Toss the dog a treat when she steps on the mark. After practicing this for a while, have the dog sitting some distance from the mark and call the dog to come to the mark ("Come, Mark"). Toss the treat when the dog is on the mark. Use different approach angles and different distances to the mark to be sure the dog really knows what it means. Gradually reduce the size of the mark. Move the mark to different places. Once your *Mark* is solid, you can use multiple marks to move the dog several times.

For actual acting work, the mark has to be invisible, so you would make it as small as a poker chip. Then you could require only one foot to be on the mark. Or you can eliminate the mark entirely, but still send the dog as if you were sending her to a mark, and use your "Stay" command to stop the dog where you want.

Timing: Be sure to reward the dog only when she is actually standing on the mark, either by tossing or handing the treat.

Command: "Mark"

Signal: Point to the mark, or, when you place it, tap the mark with your foot to be sure the dog knows where it is.

Problems: Don't let the dog "cheat the mark" by just getting near it rather than actually on it. Make sure the mark will not slip when the dog hits it. Don't be in a hurry to make the mark smaller—stay with the large, easily visible mark for a substantial amount of practice.

1. Use a large object as a mark and lure the dog onto it with a treat.

2. Make sure the dog has both front feet on the mark before giving the reward.

3. Gradually reduce the size of the mark, and call the dog to it.

4. Once the dog is hitting the mark reliably, you can ask for other behaviors while the dog is on the mark.

Diesel the Mixed Breed demonstrates Hit a mark.

LIMP

Prerequisites: *Stand, Wave*

Uses: Another behavior to elicit an emotional response . . . A limping dog just invites compassion. Work it into a storytelling routine and you're sure to impress. A behavior that might be called for in actual acting work, and one you can't train in a hurry.

Action: With your dog in a *Stand*, position yourself in front of the dog, hold out your closed hand, and wait for the dog to touch your hand with her foot. If you've already taught *Wave*, this shouldn't be a problem, but if you need a jump start, hold a treat in your hand. Always give your treat with your other hand. After a little practice, delay giving the treat to keep the dog's foot in the air for a few seconds. Next, hold your hand so the dog has to stretch to reach it. Then move your hand while the dog is touching it, to encourage the dog to hop forward. Start saying "Limp" before you present your hand. Once the dog is readily hopping a couple of steps forward, say your command and give your signal, but don't actually let the dog touch your hand. Increase distance very gradually. As you do, the dog will adjust from holding her leg out in front to tucking it up under her because it will be more comfortable.

    An alternate method is to kneel at the side of your dog, hold a treat in front of the dog, and lightly tap the back of the front leg where it bends at the wrist to get the dog to raise that leg. Then hold the treat ahead of the dog and get movement, and if the dog puts the "hurt" leg down, tap it to get it back up.

Timing: Give the treat while the dog's front leg is still in the air rather than after it's back on the ground. Do not reward if the dog has put the foot down.

Command: "Limp"

Signal: Offer your hand as though you were going to target the dog's foot to your hand.

Problems: Some dogs have a really hard time with this. They have to figure out how to move on three legs. Be patient and make changes slowly. Try moving your hand so the dog will move in a curve to follow it, rather than straight forward. So if the dog's left leg is in the air, use your left hand as the target and move it to your left. This can help her learn to adjust her weight distribution so the legs still on the ground can move. Remember that dogs are left- or right-sided, and you may do better with the opposite leg in the air.

1. Use your hand as a target to get the dog to raise a foot.

2. With your hand target keeping the dog's foot in the air, use a treat to lure the dog forward.

3. When the dog is moving a couple of steps without putting the foot down, use your cue and signal rather than having the dog target your hand.

Bobby the Mixed Breed demonstrates Limp.

FOOT TARGET

Prerequisites: Have whatever prop you want to use (piano, drum, bell)

Uses: As you can see in the photographs, you can have a musical canine orchestra, with dogs playing piano and drums, or ringing a bell. You can also have the dog turn a touch light on and off and, if you add some water-based acrylic paint, you can have your dog paint some abstract art.

Action: It will help if you have worked several behaviors that involve feet. You can try just touching the object with your hand and see if your dog responds by putting a foot on it. If not, hold a treat in your closed hand on top of your prop. Place your hand on the side of the prop closest to you so the dog will touch both your hand and the prop. While her foot is touching the prop, give a treat. After several sessions, just present the prop, without putting your hand on it, and give your command.

Or you can teach the dog to use a touch stick as a foot target. Hold the stick so the end is near your dog's foot. If you have worked on several behaviors involving feet, or used your hand as a foot target, your dog should put a foot on the touch stick with little urging. You can then use the touch stick to position the dog's foot where you want.

Once you are getting a good *Foot*, you need to be sure it is hard enough to operate your prop. So reward only more vigorous efforts. Then you need to vary how many repetitions you want, so it isn't a one-note performance. If you're using a keyboard, you also want the dog to hit different keys, so try touching different sections to get the dog to target different areas.

For painting, work outside or on copious amounts of newspaper, and don't wear your best clothes (it's messy). Be sure you're using water-based nontoxic paint. Tape a piece of art paper to a cookie sheet. Have your paints in fairly flat bowls. Dip your dog's preferred front foot into the paint, then command "Foot" to have him touch the paper.

Timing: Be sure to vary your number of repetitions so the dog will give a good performance, not play just one or two notes.

Command: "Foot," or you can name each behavior ("Play the piano," "Beat the drum," etc.)

Signal: Just point to the prop, or mime playing the piano, beating a drum.

Problems: Make sure your props won't slide or flip over and scare the dog. If your dog is really enthusiastic, you may have to secure your props to a board.

The multi-talented Bling Bling can also play the drums.

1. Get the dog warmed up with Foot touches to a touch stick or your hand.

2. Use the touch stick or your hand to position the dog's foot to hit the piano keys.

3. After some practice rely on your cue and body position to get the dog playing the instrument.

Bling Bling the Papillon demonstrates Play the piano.

BACK UP

Prerequisites: *Hit a Mark*

Uses: When you try to put distance between you and your dog, the dog tends to creep closer. *Back up* can push him back to the distance or the spot you want. Having distance between you and the dog even in a living room performance makes everything look better. *Back up* is used extensively in the sport of canine freestyle. Using a mark to help teach *Back up* avoids the "garbage truck syndrome," where the dog barks whenever backing up.

Action: Set up a chute narrow enough to keep the dog from turning around. (You can use a couch and a coffee table or dog crates.) Put a mark at one end of the chute and another mark a few feet into the chute. Have the dog standing on the mark facing out of the chute and stand in front of the dog in the opening of the chute. Give the command "Back up, Mark" and walk forward, raising your knees in an exaggerated manner to help drive the dog back. When the dog is on the end mark, reward and praise. Gradually move the marks farther apart. When the dog is moving well, make the chute wider, then get rid of it entirely. Stop moving forward, instead using your cue and body language (walk in place with exaggerated knee raises) to make the dog back up. Finally, get rid of your marks and just use the command "Back up," and when the dog is positioned where you want, tell him to "Stay."

If you choose not to teach *Hit a mark*, you can still teach *Back up*. Use an exercise pen or other objects to form a narrow V. Lure your dog into the point of the V while you stand outside the V at the point. Hold the treat behind your back. The dog, wanting to get out to get to you (and the treat), will back up because he has no other choice. As soon as he is moving, say "Back up" and toss a treat behind the dog (to make him back up farther). Once the dog backs up as soon as he is in the chute, for at least four or five feet, open up the front of the chute and then gradually move the chute away.

Timing: Don't bring the treat out until the dog is on the far mark, or it will tend to pull the dog toward you.

Command: "Back up"

Signal: Shoo the dog back with one hand.

Problems: If you don't use the chute, your dog is likely to be crooked when backing up, moving in a curve rather than straight. Don't hold the treat in front of you, as it will distract the dog. Hold it behind your back, out of sight but ready to toss. If your dog sits rather than moving, use your command "Stand." Many dogs have a tendency to bark when backing up, but using the two marks seems to keep the dog focused on a task (finding his mark) and quiet.

1. With the dog on a mark in the chute, and another mark behind the dog, walk forward with high knee lifts.

2. Once the dog is moving well, get rid of the chute but keep the marks.

3. Stop moving forward and use your cue and signal.

Diesel the Mixed Breed demonstrates Back up.

HIDE YOUR EYES

Prerequisites: *Down, Head Down*

Uses: The ultimate behavior for looking apprehensive or ashamed. A harder behavior to teach, and one that not all dogs are built to perform, so it's really impressive if you can manage it. Another fine choice to use in a storytelling routine.

Action: With the dog in a *Down*, use a hair scrunchie or a loose rubber band on the dog's muzzle. Give your command for *Head down*. It may not work right away because the dog is distracted by the object on her muzzle. You can go back to using physical manipulation if you need to. Tickle or touch the object until the dog puts a paw up to try to take the object off. Immediately remove the object and give a really good reward. Both removing the object and the treat are rewards. Start saying "Hide your eyes, Head down" after you have practiced and performance is improving.

Once the dog is readily bringing a paw up to try to remove the object from her muzzle, don't put the scrunchie or rubber band on her muzzle. Instead, ask for *Head down* and then try tickling the dog's muzzle where the object would be while saying your command "Hide your eyes." If she responds, great. If not, go back to putting the object on her muzzle for another couple of sessions.

Once you have gotten this, ask her to *Stay* in the position for a couple of seconds. Remember to use your release cue before you reward.

If you are having difficulties, you can try having the dog *On your side* rather than in *Head down* position. This makes it physically easier for the dog to put both paws over her muzzle, though it isn't quite as pretty.

Timing: When you get a good response from the dog, remove the object as quickly as possible (but gently), as that is a big part of the reward.

Command: "Hide your eyes," "Look ashamed"

Signal: Make your hands into fists and cross your forearms.

Problems: When you first put the scrunchie or rubber band on, your dog may panic. Just be patient. Reassure her and tickle or blow on the object until you get some response to try to get it off. Other dogs may stoically just be still in a resigned attitude. Often, blowing on the object will get them to swipe at it. Be sure your object isn't so tight that it's uncomfortable, or so loose that the dog can dislodge it easily. Some dogs with short legs simply can't reach their muzzle to perform this behavior.

1. Put a hair scrunchie around your dog's nose.

2. Have the dog do Head down. You may have to help him into position.

3. Tickle the scrunchie to encourage the dog to paw at it.

4. Have the dog stay in the position.

Bobby the Mixed Breed demonstrates Hide your eyes.

BALANCE A COOKIE/TOY

Prerequisites: *Sit, Stay*

Uses: A really cute trick that most dogs love performing. It will help your dog learn to catch, if this is a problem area.

Action: With your dog in a *Sit*, place a biscuit (appropriately sized for your dog) on the nose just behind the actual nose leather. At first, you may have to cup the dog's chin in your hand to help him hold his head steady. Leave the biscuit for a second, then take it off, and reward with a second treat. After a few sessions, with the dog steady for a couple of seconds, move on to the second part of the behavior.

Give your command "Catch it" or "Flip it" in an excited tone of voice and the dog will probably react by going for the cookie. If the biscuit drops to the floor, don't let the dog have it, but don't be negative about it (no yelling "No!") or the dog won't want to play the game. The dog gets the flipped biscuit only if he catches it in the air. Have patience—it may take him a while to get this one. Practice just the balancing part in between tries so that the dog gets rewarded.

Timing: You will have to be on your toes to get to any dropped treats before your dog does.

Command: "Catch it," "Flip it"

Signal: Snap your fingers

Problems: If the dog drops the cookie, make sure you get to it before the dog. Use your foot to cover it if you have to. If your dog is bad at catching the cookie, it may help to teach the dog to catch as a separate behavior. If he's very bad at catching, having him stand on the end of a picnic table so the treat drops to the ground if he doesn't catch it. This gives you a better chance of not letting the dog have any dropped cookies.

Diesel the Mixed Breed demonstrates Balance a cookie.

1. Place the biscuit across your dog's nose and help him hold steady.

2. Take the biscuit away and give a treat with your other hand.

3. Have the dog balance the biscuit on his own.

4. Cue the dog to flip the biscuit.

CHAPTER 12
THE PLOT LINE

You and your dog have now learned a whole variety of exciting new behaviors. You're probably enjoying showing them off. Your audience is probably deeply impressed. But you can do more.

When you teach a complicated behavior or combine behaviors into a storytelling sequence, you break it down into separate pieces, train each one, and then put them together. This is called chaining. In teaching *Say your prayers*, you chain several behaviors together to create a new behavior. Now we're going to chain behaviors to tell a story.

Choose five or six behaviors your dog does well. Now, think of how you can put those behaviors together to tell a story.

Say, for example, your dog does well at *Speaking, Playing dead, Crawling,* and *Taking a bow.* Watch how these behaviors combine to tell a war story.

We need a mission. How about a member of the underground bringing critical information back from the front? And of course there has to be a bad guy. Now for some details.

Every good dog should *Say his prayers* before going off to war. (Extend your arm and cue him to "Pray.") You never know if you're coming back. His superior officer (you) then orders him to the front to retrieve critical information from an underground informant. (Have a helper call your dog unobtrusively.)

Canine special agent makes his rendezvous with his contact and receives the critical information. The informant then points the canine agent back to base camp. While hurrying back, the brave agent encounters a bad guy. He's shot and left for dead. (Call him back to you, but give your "Bang" signal as the "bad guy" shoots him.) But he was only wounded, and manages to drag himself in a painful *Crawl* back to his superior officer. (Cue him to crawl to you.) With his last breath, he's able to bark out the critical information necessary to save the troops. (Cue "Speak.") But, alas, the effort was too much for him and he collapses. (Give your "Bang" signal again.) But don't worry—canine special agent recuperated in a rehabilitation hospital and is doing just fine. (Have him jump up and take a *Bow.*)

Okay, maybe it's silly. But you can come up with your own story. Whatever story you're using, it's important that people understand what's going on or it might not make much sense. So deliver a little spiel before the action, something like this:

"Canine special agent is a member of the underground during World War I. His mission is to reach a contact across enemy lines and bring back critical information. He stands a good chance of being shot, but he'll do his best to make it back. And because the mission is so dangerous, he'll say a prayer before he goes."

One place to get ideas from is your television. Dogs are very popular in advertising and film, and you'll probably see at least one in any given series of commercial breaks or as a regular on a TV show. If you see a dog doing something you'd like to train your dog to do, think about how the behavior might have been accomplished. And some movies feature dogs as the lead—lots of ideas for you.

We hope that you have received great enjoyment from this book and that you and your dog will bond even more closely through training these behaviors. Most dogs are show-offs at heart, and enjoy being in the spotlight. Share your dog's new abilities so everyone can enjoy them.

USEFUL ADDRESSES

United States Department of Agriculture (USDA)
APHIS Animal Care Headquarters
4700 River Road, Unit 84
Riverdale, MD 20737-1234
301/734-7833 (phone)
301/734-4978 (fax)
www.aphis.usda.gov
E-mail: Ace@aphis.usda.gov

Western Region
USDA/APHIS/Animal Care
2150 Centre Avenue
Building B, Mailstop 3W11
Fort Collins, CO 80526-8117
970/494-7478 (phone)
970/494-7461 (fax)
E-mail: Acwest@aphis.usda.gov

Eastern Region
USDA/APHIS/Animal Care
920 Main Campus Drive
Suite 200
Raleigh, NC 27606-5210
919/855-7100 (phone)
919/855-7123 (fax)
E-mail: Aceast@aphis.usda.gov

LA411
5700 Wilshire Boulevard, Suite 12
Los Angeles, CA 90036
800/545-2411
www.la411.com
New York Office
360 Park Avenue South, 17th Floor
New York, NY 10010
646/746-6891

The Creative Handbook
North American Edition
10152 Riverside Drive
Toluca Lake, CA 91602
818/752-3200 (phone)
www.creativehandbook.com

Therapy Dogs International
88 Bartley Road
Flanders, NJ 07836
973/252-9800
www.tdi-dog.org
E-mail: Tdi@gti.net

Therapy Dogs, Inc.
P.O. Box 20227
Cheyenne, WY 82003
877/843-7364
www.therapydogs.com
E-mail: Therapydogsinc@qwestoffice.net

Angel on a Leash
244 Fifth Avenue, #2312
New York, NY 10001
877/364-2643
www.angelonaleash.org
E-mail: Info@angelonaleash.org

Delta Society
875 124th Avenue NE, Suite 101
Bellevue, WA 98005
425/679-5500
www.deltasociety.org
E-mail: Info@deltasociety.org

Association of Pet Dog Trainers
150 Executive Center Drive
Box 35
Greenville, SC 29615
800-PET-DOGS (800/738-3647)
www.apdt.com
E-mail: Information@apdt.com

World Canine Freestyle Organization
3050 Pratt Lane
Attica, MI 48412
646/812-7067
www.worldcaninefreestyle.org
E-mail: allpurposedog@yahoo.com

GLOSSARY

Agility: an organized dog sport in which dogs negotiate a course comprised of jumps, tunnels, and other obstacles

Bait bag: a small pouch attached to a belt or waistband for holding treats

Bar jump: a jump consisting of a bar supported on stanchions

Bending: a flexibility exercise in which the dog is encouraged to flex his or her spine; also a term for performance of the agility weave poles

Canine freestyle: an organized dog sport in which dog and handler perform a choreographed routine to music, using obedience, trick training, jumping, etc.

Chaining: combining small components of a behavior into a whole performance, or combining separate behaviors into a sequence

Clicker training: training using a small noisemaker as a cue to the dog; the dog is taught to associate the sound with a food reward, and the clicker is then clicked at the precise moment that the dog is performing some desired behavior

Conformation: an organized dog sport in which dogs are judged on their physical makeup against a written standard of perfection for their breed

Crawl tunnel: an obstacle in agility, which the dog must crawl through

Drives: a dog's motivational components; a dog chasing a ball is in prey drive, imitating the chasing of prey; a dog drooling over the meatloaf on the kitchen counter is in food drive

Flyball: an organized dog sport in which teams of dogs relay race over a series of hurdles, catch a ball propelled out of a box, and return over the hurdles

Intermittent reward: a reward offered sporadically (an example of a powerful intermittent reward in the context of human experience is the payoff from a slot machine—this expected payoff can keep a person gambling)

Lure: food or a toy used as an enticement to get a dog to move into the desired position

Obedience: an organized dog sport in which dogs perform a series of exercises including heeling, standing, coming when called, and staying in a sit and down; more advanced levels include retrieving and off-leash work

Pet therapy: bringing dogs to visit those in hospitals or convalescent hospitals in order to cheer them up

Play bow: a natural behavior, in which the dog lowers his front end to the ground with his rear in the air, used to induce another dog (or human) to play

Pretraining: work done before an acting assignment in order to have the dog perform some difficult piece of behavior specifically requested

Prey drive: a basic motivation calling on the dog's hunting instinct; herding dogs exhibit a strong prey drive but stop short of actually making the "kill"

Puppy push-ups: an aerobic exercise in which the dog is commanded to sit, down, sit, down repeatedly

Reach: the extension of the dog's forelegs out in front of the dog when moving, especially at a trot

Recall: the "Come" command, wherein the dog will stop whatever he or she is doing and return to the handler

School visit programs: educational programs in which an owner brings a dog to school and discusses care and training and how to behave around dogs

Search and rescue: activities of trained dog/handler teams using the dog's scenting abilities to find lost people or those trapped in disaster areas

Shaping: developing a behavior by accepting a small step toward the behavior at first and gradually demanding performance closer to the full behavior

Stack: in the conformation ring, the display of the dog in a standing position, in which the dog's feet must be carefully placed to show the dog off to best advantage

Tab: a short, three- to five-inch piece of leather or nylon that can be attached to the dog's collar to offer a convenient handle for correcting or controlling the dog

Traffic leash: a short, typically three-foot leash, meant to keep the dog under close control

Weave poles: an agility obstacle, which the dog performs by zig-zagging through a series of poles spaced along a line